THE GOSPEL OF THOMAS

THE GOSPEL OF THOMAS

A GUIDEBOOK FOR SPIRITUAL PRACTICE

Ron Miller

Walking Together, Finding the Way
SKYLIGHT PATHS Publishing
Woodstock, Vermont

The Gospel of Thomas:
A Guidebook for Spiritual Practice

2004 First Printing

Library of Congress Cataloging-in-Publication Data
Miller, Ron, 1938–
The Gospel of Thomas : a guidebook for spiritual practice / Ron Miller.
p. cm.
Includes bibliographical references.
ISBN 1-59473-047-4 (pbk.)
1. Gospel of Thomas (Coptic Gospel)—Criticism, interpretation, etc.
2. Spiritual life. I. Title.
BS2860.T52M54 2004
229'.8—dc22 2004006361

10 9 8 7 6 5 4 3 2 1
Manufactured in the United States of America
Cover Design: Sara Dismukes
Cover Art: Mummy portrait from Egypt. Wax tempera painting on wood. A young man in Roman dress and contemporary hair and beard style. Members of the Greco-Roman upper class, who adopted the Egyptian custom of mummification, had an image of themselves incorporated over the face of the mummy. Used by permission of Staatliche Antikensammlungen und Glyptothek, München.

SkyLight Paths Publishing is creating a place where people of different spiritual traditions come together for challenge and inspiration, a place where we can help each other understand the mystery that lies at the heart of our existence.

SkyLight Paths sees both believers and seekers as a community that increasingly transcends traditional boundaries of religion and denomination—people wanting to learn from each other, *walking together, finding the way.*

Walking Together, Finding the Way
Published by SkyLight Paths Publishing
A Division of LongHill Partners, Inc.
Sunset Farm Offices, Route 4, P.O. Box 237
Woodstock, VT 05091
Tel: (802) 457-4000 Fax: (802) 457-4004
www.skylightpaths.com

In honor of Elizabeth Werrenrath
my colleague, my student, my teacher, and my friend
on her ninetieth birthday

CONTENTS

INTRODUCTION

Einstein once remarked that after the dropping of the atomic bombs on Hiroshima and Nagasaki in 1945, everything had changed but our way of thinking. It is more than a coincidence that in that same year a book buried for centuries was found in Egypt, a book we know as the Gospel of Thomas.[1] From the time I first read it, I felt that it answered Einstein's concern. Here was a book that could actually change our way of thinking.

There are many academic commentaries on the Gospel of Thomas but this book has a different aim. It is meant to be a guidebook, that is, a translation of the sayings into daily practice. The goal of such practice is to become Jesus's twin. This does not, of course, mean becoming an olive-skinned, bearded Mediterranean peasant wearing sandals. It is more about manifesting in our lives the same Christ consciousness revealed in the person we know as Jesus of Nazareth. This image of the twin goes back to the very first words of the Gospel of Thomas: "These are the hidden sayings that the living Jesus spoke and that Didymus Judas Thomas wrote down." Now this could simply be a reference to the apostle who in other texts is known as Thomas. But a deeper meaning could lie in the fact that the names Thomas in Aramaic and Didymus in Greek both mean *twin*.

It must be clear from the outset, however, that being Jesus's twin does not imply membership in any of the churches in today's religious landscape calling themselves Christian. This teaching, like all the most profound spiritual teachings, is for everyone. One need no more be a Christian to benefit from what this volume contains than one need be a Buddhist to learn from the Buddha's Four Noble Truths or a Muslim to be inspired by the Five Pillars of Islam. May we all be Buddha's twin, Moses's twin, and Muhammad's twin as well. May we all come from the world's womb as the spiritual twin of every great teacher and mystic. For in the essence of what they individually manifest, these great teachers are all one.

I speak of *becoming* Jesus's twin rather than *being* Jesus's twin. The process is primary, the way more important than the goal, the striving more important than the achievement. Carving words in stone makes sense only after a person is dead. I am suspicious of any religious expression in the past tense. I cannot believe in a reform*ed* church, an "I *found* it" bumper sticker, or a *closed* canon of revelation, implying that God can no longer speak. Becoming a Thomas Believer, a twin of Jesus, means entering on a path that will end only with our last breath, and perhaps not even then.

Becoming is our nature. End points, closed systems, neat definitions—these simply do not fit the human condition. I refer often in my teaching and writing to "the three Ps." All our knowledge is partial, provisional, and perspectival. What we know is only a part and there are others with parts completing the picture we are trying to see. What we know is provisional; it always needs revision. What we know is perspectival. We cannot fully escape seeing things from our own perspective: as a man or a woman, someone poor or someone rich, someone gay or someone straight.

Becoming a Thomas Believer has been a journey for me. That journey falls into two parts that can best be demarcated as "Before Thomas" and "After Thomas." Raised a Roman Catholic, I entered the Society of Jesus (the Jesuits) when I was seventeen and spent twenty years as a Jesuit. I was still a Jesuit when I began my doctoral work in comparative religions at Northwestern University, but I was no longer a Jesuit when I received my doctorate in 1978. I had left the Jesuits and the clerical priesthood in 1975, the year that would forever after be the year one A.T. (After Thomas) in my life's calendar.

That same year, 1975, I cofounded Common Ground, an organization for religious study and dialogue corresponding to the vision of the world that I had imbibed in my doctoral work in comparative religions. In my personal journey as a Christian, I found religious pluralism most consonant with my own experience. The Anglican theologian Alan Race introduced a threefold way of considering other religions: exclusivism, inclusivism, and pluralism. The Harvard theologian Diana Eck has developed this model and made it popular in interreligious dialogue.[2]

Exclusivism is the belief that all religious truth lives within one tradition and, therefore, anything outside that tradition is wrong. This is the position of fundamentalists of every stripe. The second option, inclusivism, holds that there is truth in other sacred traditions, but the fullness of truth is embodied in only one of these, one's own. This has been the official position of Roman Catholicism since the Second Vatican Council in the 1960s. Pluralism stems from the hypothesis that if one religion is true, then all religions are probably true. This approach sees the diversity of religions as somewhat parallel to the diversity of languages. There are different ways of articulating the divine mystery and different paths leading to it.

As a Christian, I found two primary roadblocks to being a pluralist. First, there is the normative Christian teaching of the unique character of Jesus. If he is the "only begotten Son of the Father" then there is simply nothing comparable in any other religion. Second, if, in order to be saved, we must be explicitly connected with Jesus's atoning death for the ravages of original sin, how can one be open to other religions as potentially just as true as one's own? I came to resolve these conundrums in my own life and theology when I realized that there were other forms of Christianity that understood Jesus's uniqueness in a different way and rejected the theology both of original sin and of an atoning death. The Gospel of Thomas articulates a first-century form of precisely such an alternative Christian theology.

Neither original sin nor atoning death appears in the Gospel of Thomas's 114 sayings attributed to Jesus. The Gospel of Thomas helps us to realize that there has been an alternative sense of being Christian all along, a more mystical kind of Christian tradition that has usually been hidden and often been persecuted by the larger Church. And yet, whispers of it are heard in the Christian Testament, in other Christian writings through the centuries, and especially in the testimony of the mystics. This hidden current is emerging once again in our own day in the writings of scholars such as Matthew Fox, Bishop John Shelby Spong, Marcus Borg, Karen King, and Elaine Pagels.

But isn't the Gospel of Thomas gnostic and heretical? Having read every book on gnosticism that I could get my hands on, I concluded with a sense of defeat that I simply couldn't grasp its unifying reality. Then it occurred to me that perhaps the reason I couldn't perceive its unifying reality was that it didn't have one. In other words, maybe gnosticism is no more than a convenient term, covering diverse religious movements, a label used by "orthodox" Christians to classify any group they regarded as heretical.[3] Calling the Gospel of Thomas gnostic may be no more than a way of saying that it is different from the forms of Christianity that have been dominant for most of Christian history.

All of this constituted my own path in becoming a Thomas Believer. But, as I stated earlier, Thomas Believers today come from many spiritual homes and backgrounds. They may be Hindus or Buddhists, Jews or Muslims. Today's newly emergent Thomas Believers are not organized in any fashion in the contemporary religious landscape. Any formal organization, especially a hierarchical one, would be foreign and even repellent to Thomas Believers. So too would be a set of rules or prescribed rituals.

My reading of the Gospel of Thomas may not be that of other scholars in the field and may even disagree with what the original author (or authors) intended. After all, one of the difficulties of this text is that we have teachings without context. There are many times when the reader simply does not know to whom the pronouns are referring. Furthermore, there is much that is enigmatic or obscure in these 114 statements attributed to Jesus. Nevertheless, my current understanding of the text (and I look forward to being corrected by my readers) describes for me a form of spirituality closest to what I have reached at this point in my journey. This guidebook, in the last analysis, is no more than an expression of my own self-discovery, my own spiritual path as a Thomas Believer, and my own attempt to become a spiritual adult.

I am grateful to SkyLight Paths for inviting me to write this volume. I would call it a coincidence, except that I do not think there are any coincidences. I was studying at home when I received a call from Maura Shaw of SkyLight Paths Publishing. I had just purchased and begun to read that publisher's edition of *The Gospel of Thomas,* as translated and annotated by Stevan Davies, and here was Maura asking me if I would be interested in writing a guidebook on this same text. Within forty-eight hours of her call, I had written a substantial part of the text. So my first thanks goes to SkyLight Paths.

My life is constantly nourished by a network of support communities, among them Common Ground, Lake Forest College, and the Interreligious Engagement Project 21. My thanks go to all the wonderful people who make these associations vibrant and creative. I am also grateful to Jim and Carrie, my son and daughter, for the brightness of their lives and their ability to bring so much joy to my work and to my life.

PRELUDE

The Faith of a Thomas Believer

I believe in one God, a divine mystery
beyond all definition and rational understanding,
the heart of all that has ever existed,
that exists now, or that ever will exist.

I believe in Jesus, messenger of God's Word,
bringer of God's healing, heart of God's compassion,
bright star in the firmament of God's
prophets, mystics, and saints.

I believe in the Holy Spirit,
the life of God that is our innermost life,
the breath of God moving in our being,
the depth of God living in each of us.

I believe that I am called to be Jesus's twin,
allowing myself to be a vehicle of God's love,
a source of God's wisdom and truth,
and an instrument of God's peace in the world.

I believe that God's reign is here and now,
stretched out all around us for those

with eyes to see it, hearts to receive it,
and hands to make it happen.

I believe in the community of God seekers
in all the religions, as well as outside of them,
the great prophets, mystics, and saints,
and those just beginning their spiritual journey.

I believe in a future on this earth when all
will be God-centered and God-conscious,
when we will learn to live in love and peace,
in the fellowship of brothers and sisters.

I believe that in death, life is changed,
not taken away, and that we will go
from step to step in God's life, God's love,
and God's glory for all eternity. Amen.

1

Becoming a Spiritual Adult

WHO COMES TO MIND IF I ASK YOU TO THINK OF THE PEOPLE YOU consider to be whole and holy? At the Parliament of the World's Religions that met in Capetown, South Africa, in 1999, I recall a lunch hosted by the mayor of Capetown after an address by the Dalai Lama. I was sitting with a Wiccan from Wisconsin and she said to me, "The Dalai Lama is an adult. That's refreshing." At first, I didn't grasp the implications of what she had said. Then I realized how insightful her comment was. We live in a world largely run by children—and here I mean childish people, not childlike people. The daily newspapers show us the tragedies of playground conduct elevated to the level of armies and governments.

I was preparing for class one day at Common Ground, the adult education center I cofounded twenty-nine years ago, when I heard loud honking outside. I opened the door and looked outside. It was winter and the area was blanketed with snow. The snowplows had cleared only one lane in the street. Two cars had met head on and were loudly honking at each other. Now there were shoveled driveways on both sides of the street, so the problem could easily have been resolved by one car simply backing into a driveway to let the other pass by. But they chose to remain there, bumper to bumper, honking at each other. Then both drivers, a man and a woman, got out of their respective cars and started screaming at each other. I shut the door in disbelief and went back to my class preparation.

What a parable this provides for most of what we find in our newspapers. We read about the deadly cycle of retaliation of Israelis and Palestinians, neither party able to rise above the schoolyard behavior of ten-year-olds. Our own government operates at a tribal level of consciousness, assigning people white hats or black hats: "the coalition of the willing" and "the axis of evil." National politics resembles the cowboy movies I watched as a child, when all problems were resolved with a "shootout." It's frightening to realize that there are no adults on the job. Small wonder that we are so delighted to meet an adult like the Dalai Lama.

What adults do you know? You might want to take a few minutes to make a list. Such a list might include Jesus and the Mary called Magdalene, Moses and Muhammad, Hildegard of Bingen and Francis of Assisi, Teresa of Ávila and Thich Nhat Hanh, the Buddha and the Baal Shem Tov, Rumi and Ramakrishna, Martin Luther King Jr. and Mahatma Gandhi, Thomas Merton and Dorothy Day. It's good to realize that our planet has produced adults. It's good to look at pictures of adults, to read their writings, to remember their lives.

I grew up with the Roman Catholic calendar, where there was a saint for every day. Perhaps it's time for a new calendar of adults, people of all religions and of none, who reached holiness and wholeness. Remember to keep one page on that calendar, one date in that year, for yourself. If we don't feel that we deserve to be there yet, it can still be our goal, what we trust that we are becoming. It's good to become an adult before we die.

1 And he said: Whoever finds the correct interpretation of these sayings will never die.

The words of Jesus in the Gospel of Thomas seem to imply that the chief characteristic of a spiritual adult is finding the deeper self that does not die. If we understand these sayings and are truly transformed by their wisdom, then we will know that depth in ourselves that is deathless. This is a considerable promise, and what is most characteristic of the Gospel of Thomas is that wisdom comes from our activity, our finding the correct interpretation, not from an outside agent, someone or something that gives us immortality.

> **2 Jesus said: The seeker should not stop until he finds. When he does find, he will be disturbed. After having been disturbed, he will be astonished. Then he will reign over everything.**

The canonical gospels talk about seeking and finding. What is distinct in this saying is that finding is not the end of it. There follow disturbance, astonishment, and ruling. The simple and perhaps simplistic seeking/finding model informs much of ordinary Christianity. "I found it." "I once was lost but now am found." Here in the Gospel of Thomas, the finding is but one stage in a more nuanced and sophisticated process.

Why, if we have found something, should we be disturbed? Because we realize that what we have found fails to bring us closure, calling us instead to yet another challenge. There's a great deal in the Gospel of Thomas's message that is disturbing. The fact that we need to save ourselves. The fact that Jesus does not want our worship but our work. The fact that, ultimately, everything is God. All of this pushes us beyond the comfort zone of ordinary religion. This pushes Christians beyond the comfort of taking refuge in Jesus, his saving blood, his atoning death, and his inexplicable choice to save a few of us, despite our unworthiness. It pushes others beyond the comfort of the mercy of the Buddha, the wisdom of the guru, the power of the crystal, the assurance of the infallible teacher, the comfort of the inerrant text. In every instance, there is a call to grow up, to take responsibility, to be an adult.

But once we have passed that stage of disturbance, we are astonished. How extraordinary to come to realize our true identity, our incredible power, and our rightful heritage. At that point, we truly come to rule. Not, of course, in the sense of manipulation or dominance, but in the healthy sense of being in control, not cringing before an angry God, a demanding hierarchy, or a frightening roulette game of predestination. We reach a calm and peaceful place of control, no longer victims of the whims of cult leaders or horoscopes. We have realized our inherent dignity as daughters and sons of God, beings who are divine to our core, loved beyond measure, able to make a difference in a playground world looking around anxiously for grown-ups. We are finally home. We are finally adults.

> **3b When you understand yourselves you will be understood. And you will realize that you are Sons of the living Father. If you do not know yourselves, then you exist in poverty and you are that poverty.**

When we truly understand ourselves, then we can be understood by others. We speak and act with the authority of self-authenticating experience. We possess that interior wealth that thieves cannot steal nor moths or rust consume. Without this understanding, we are indeed poor. How poor are those anxiously waiting in fear to see if some "holy father" approves of them, or if some text of an inerrant book confirms the truth of their experience, or if their life fits someone else's definitions or someone else's rules.

> **24 His disciples said to him: Show us the place you are, for it is essential for us to seek it. He responded: He who has ears let him hear. There is light within a man of light, and he lights up all of the world. If he is not alight there is darkness.**

Again we see this natural seeking of external confirmation. We want "Father" to tell us it's right. We want "the good book" to give us a text on which to hang our fate. It's hard to grow up and be an adult, to take responsibility for our own actions and our own lives. There is a story about Pope John XXIII. Whether it is true or not, I cannot say. Shortly after he was elected pope, he woke up with a question on his mind and a spontaneous instinct prompted him to say, "I've got to see the pope about this." But then, as he fully awoke from sleep, he thought to himself, "Wait a minute. I am the pope." Fortunately, John XXIII was a man who could live with waking up to his own identity. For he was a man of light and that's why he found the courage to open the windows so that light could shine on his severely dysfunctional church. Unfortunately, those who followed him are working fast to nail all those windows shut again.

58 Jesus said: Blessed is one who has labored and has found life.

This saying is crucial for its reiteration of a central theme of the Gospel of Thomas. We must labor to find life. We must be adults. We must take responsibility for our spiritual growth. Our salvation is not going to happen without us. For far too long, Christians have been obsessed with this notion that "all is grace" and "all is faith" and there's no room for works. That is one of the most damaging pieces of nonsense ever foisted on spiritual seekers. Ignatius of Loyola admonished his companions to pray as if everything depended on God but to work as if everything depended on them. In the spiritual life there is far too much laziness passing itself off as trust in God.

41 Jesus said: Whoever possesses some will be given more. Whoever possesses virtually nothing will have what little he does possess taken away.

A very adult message is embedded in this teaching. Growth doesn't just happen to us. Some sixty-year-olds have had sixty years of experience; others have had one year of experience sixty times. We have to take advantage of the opportunity that is there. If we lose it, we lose all the consequences it would have given birth to; but if we grasp it, we gain all the consequences following from it.

As soon as we take the first step—like waking up half an hour earlier for some kind of spiritual practice—doors start to open up. A book attracts our attention or a retreat or a spiritual workshop. Soon we are part of a meditation group or a book club discussing spiritual literature. On the other hand, when we have virtually nothing going on in our spiritual practice, soon even that little bit disappears. Growing up spiritually is going to take some effort, even some skill.

42 Be one of those who pass by.

This is the shortest teaching attributed to Jesus from all the teachings we have in early Christian literature. And yet, its profundity more than makes up for its brevity. Jesus lived in this world literally as a homeless person, sleeping outside on many occasions, eating when kindly women provided him with food. The Thomas Believer is not necessarily called to a literal imitation of Jesus in this regard. But at a profoundly existential level, every Thomas Believer must be homeless. All spiritual adults are passersby. A Chinese adage reminds us that life is a bridge. We should pass over it but not try to build our house on it.

The Second Noble Truth of the Buddha teaches us that clinging is the source of all our suffering. If we can let go of that clinging, of that inordinate attachment, of that delusional goal of stopping life from being transitory, then we can let go of all our self-generated suffering and experience an adult life of joy and peace. That's why the Buddha teaches that everything is on fire. It's like the game of "hot potato" we played as children. We need to throw the ball to someone else as soon as we catch it. We can hold things only briefly, for we need to know how to let them go. Otherwise, they will inevitably burn us.

There is a story of a young man who goes to a Buddhist teacher and asks for insight into the Second Noble Truth. The teacher picks up the small drinking glass on the table where she is sitting. "Do you see this glass?" she asks. "Yes," says the young man. "Well, for me the glass is already broken; and that's why I can enjoy drinking from it and take pleasure in seeing the sunlight dance on its surface." The glass is already broken. What does that mean? It means that the teacher understands the transience of all earthly reality. Far from being saddened, because she accepts it, she can enjoy all that passes through her hands. Here was someone who understood what it means to be a passerby.

Practice

A Buddhist retreat I attended years ago began with the roshi saying: "Take half an hour to do anything you want, but do it with attention." There is another story of someone asking a spiritual teacher for the first lesson of spiritual growth. Her answer was "Attention." Somewhat disappointed at the apparent banality of the answer, the questioner persisted. "What's the second lesson?" "Attention," said the teacher. "And the third lesson?" "Attention."

Nothing happens without attention. I'm sure that many people brushed past the Buddha as they were hurrying to the marketplace for the latest sale. Others must have been impatient hearing Jesus talk because they had a "hot date" that evening. Others listened to Muhammad and then shouted at him to get out of town because his constant teaching about taking care of the poor was making them feel uncomfortable about their own shady business practices. It makes no difference if Buddha, Jesus, or Muhammad is teaching if no one is paying attention.

For the next half hour, don't do anything different. Just do what you were planning to do after finishing the first chapter of this book. But do it with attention. If you're sitting, pay attention to how your body feels. Are there places of tension and stress? If you get up to walk to the kitchen, pay attention to how your feet feel on the floor, to the water you're pouring into the kettle for the cup of tea you are making for yourself. Are you looking out the window? What are you seeing? Are you taking a cup from the shelf? How does it feel in your hands? Practice this for half an hour and then reflect on the practice.

Reflections

1. Do I often find that I've done things on automatic pilot? I ate lunch but don't remember what I ate? I arrive at home

but don't remember driving there? I read thirty pages of a book but don't remember anything I read?

2. Does it make a difference when I pay attention? Do things feel different? Does it help a bit to be where I am? Does it feel good to be where I am?
3. What happens when I don't pay attention? Do I rush out the door only to have to return because I forgot my car keys? Do I put the cat in the refrigerator and set the milk carton on the chair?

2

Making Life All of a Piece

45a Jesus said: They do not pick grapes from brambles, nor do they pick figs from thistles, for these do not bear fruit.

45b A good man brings good things out of his storehouse, but a bad man brings bad things from his storehouse (which is in his heart). And he says bad things. For out of the surplus in his heart he brings out bad things.

My father was Protestant, my mother Catholic. As a young exclusivist Catholic, I prayed frequently for my father's conversion. By the time he died at ninety-five, I realized that I needed to pray for my own conversion. Once while visiting New York, my family attended Mass at St. Patrick's Cathedral. It was a Solemn High Mass and Cardinal Spellman was presiding. I turned to my father and asked him if this wasn't enough to prompt his conversion. He simply turned to me with a smile and said, "I don't recall Jesus saying much about ritual, but he did say something about knowing a tree by its fruits." This left me with quite a conundrum to ponder, one that I didn't fully unpack for another fifty years. Ritual doesn't mean much unless it matches life and is all of a piece with it.

46a Jesus said: From Adam to John the Baptist, no one born of a woman is above John the Baptist, so that he should not lower his eyes.

46b But I have said: Whoever among you becomes like an infant will know the Kingdom and be greater than John.

Jesus had great respect for John the Baptist, the Jewish prophet who was both his teacher and his mentor. It was John the Baptist who first taught him to proclaim God's Kingdom. But John's sense of God's Kingdom was still tied to a future time when the record would be set straight by a fiery divine intervention. At some point, perhaps after John's death, Jesus grew to grasp a different sense of God's reign, the one we find central to these teachings. It is not through the calculation of calendars that we will know this Kingdom, the kind of pseudotheology found in the series of popular books by Jenkins and LaHaye.[4] It is the infant who will know the mystery of God's reign. Rather than reflecting a schism between now and then, spiritual time is all of a piece.

Why an infant? Because an infant has so little experience that the grids of prejudice have not yet been formed to block the perception of what is there in front of him. Recently two alums of the college where I teach came to see me with their two-year-old son. The little boy rushed into my living room and then came to a dramatic halt. He stood there staring at everything and everyone around him. What I would give to have eyes to see as he saw. These are the kinds of eyes that can see the Kingdom. That's why one of the most repeated statements in Jesus's teaching is this: Let those who have eyes to see, see; let those who have ears to hear, hear.

47a Jesus said: One person cannot ride two horses at once, nor stretch two bows,

47b nor can a servant serve two masters, as he will respect one and despise the other.

The Letter of James (Jesus's brother, Jacob) was probably written by some of his disciples after his death but nonetheless contains teachings going back to this man who led the Jerusalem Church for over thirty years. In this letter (James 1:8) we are told that "the doubter, being double-minded and unstable in every way, must not expect to receive anything from the Lord." It is this double-mindedness that is being highlighted in this teaching. It stands in contrast to the purity of heart that Jesus praises in Matthew 5:8. As the Danish religious thinker Søren Kierkegaard reminds us: Purity of heart means to will one thing.

The examples Jesus cites are graphic. One appears in the canonical gospels (serving two masters) but the other two (riding two horses, stretching two bows) appear only here. We pride ourselves today on multitasking. Just this morning I saw a man at my gym riding his stationary bicycle while listening to his Walkman and reading the *Wall Street Journal.* What elaborate methods we have devised for never being in the here and now, never really being focused. This is why we can't see the ways in which our lives are pulled in two contrary directions. The same popular magazine describes weight-loss programs while providing recipes for calorie-filled desserts. We go to church on Sunday but worship money as our greatest good. We say we love our children but we never make the time to be with them. We weep over the environmental plunder of our planet and then console ourselves by buying a Hummer.

Practice

Paul Tillich, a great twentieth-century theologian, spoke of our Ultimate Concern. Let me suggest an experiment here as a form of practice. Think of what you are doing right now and ask yourself why you are doing it. "I'm reading this book because a friend told me I might learn something from it." "And what are you trying to learn?" "A little more about living a spiritual life." "And why do you want more of a spiritual life?" "Because I think life is more than my job and what's on TV." "And why do you want that more abundant life?" "Because that's the best way to be." Fine. Now turn around, kneel down, and worship. You have found your god, because you have found your Ultimate Concern: abundant life. Not a bad Ultimate Concern to have!

Of course, the experiment could end with different results. You might end up with money as your god, or power, popularity, sex, or pleasure. It takes discernment to sift through the many things we do until we find our real master, for that Ultimate Concern cannot be more than one. If we are ruthlessly honest, however, we will eventually come to understand what we truly worship. We can only hope that it will be something truly ultimate, worthy of our adoration, our life's dedication, our heart's service.

Reflections

1. Do I sometimes feel as if I were trying to ride two horses? Is my multitasking becoming insanely hectic?
2. Can I apply Kierkegaard's norm—that purity of heart is to will one thing? Imagine what one thing you could will in all the diverse activities of an ordinary day.
3. Just as I might check my blood pressure periodically or my weight, can I do an "Ultimate Concern" test now and then during my week?

3

Sorting Out the Old and the New

47c No one drinks vintage wine and immediately wants to drink fresh wine.

47d Fresh wine is not put into old wineskins because they might burst. Vintage wine is not put into new wineskins because it might be spoiled.

47e A patch of old cloth is not sewn onto a new garment because it would tear.

JESUS KNEW THAT WHAT HE WAS TEACHING WAS NOT SIMPLY A REHASH OF the standard fare of organized religion at his time. It's not only that his teachings did not articulate typical Judaism in the first century. Those teachings would be equally foreign to typical Christianity or typical Buddhism or typical Islam today. For Jesus was teaching a mystical awareness that, while undergirding all the great traditions, eludes their exoteric identity, that is, the external face of religion dealing only with surface realities.

Would Thomas Believers be accepted by most Jews, Christians, Muslims, Buddhists, or Hindus today? I think not. Too much has been invested in the forms and formulas of current religion. Too much is at stake for those who wield religion to gain political control over other people or even over whole countries. Too much would be risked for those who see the purpose of religion as keeping people at a level of spiritual infantilism, providing them with a nursery world filled with nostalgia and childhood comfort foods.

> **55 Jesus said: He who doesn't hate his father and mother cannot be a disciple of mine. He who doesn't hate his brothers and sisters and bear his cross as I do will not be worthy of me.**

Since this text can also be found in the canonical gospels, we find countless commentaries reminding us of the outlandish hyperbole so common in Middle Eastern discourse. Jesus is talking about priorities, not about literally hating others, especially the very parents we are enjoined to honor by one of the Ten Commandments. And yet, I think we must be cautious in declawing this teaching.

Families are sometimes hazardous to our health. They can function like the "old wineskins" in the last saying. They often represent change-resistant habits. "This is how we've always done it." As parents, we have strong ego hooks into our children. Something in us wants them to replicate us (which is why we often give them our name with the addition of a "junior" or "the second"). We might want them to carry on our business or adhere to our religion or continue to live in our town or vote in our party. And this is dangerous. This is ego.

I once heard the very spiritual Brother David Steindl-Rast speak at Loyola University. A woman from the audience expressed concern that her children were not going to church with her anymore. He made an interesting distinction. He said that wanting our children to have a spiritual path is laudable. But wanting them to have *our* spiritual path is ego. The same would apply to all our dreams for our children. We need to untie those bonds of ego in which we seek to entrap them and they, for their part, need to be wary of us, maintaining a healthy distance when necessary.

> **56 Jesus said: Whoever has known the world has found a corpse; whoever has found that corpse, the world is not worthy of him.**

I understand "the world" in the Gospel of Thomas not as the world of flowers and sunshine, but as the socialized world. It certainly makes sense that our socialized world is a corpse, as dead and lifeless as King Midas's daughter turned to gold by the touch of her greedy father's hands. The socialized world is always old; the formulas defining it are outdated by the time they are discovered. But the world constantly being called into being by God is ever new.

I believe that Stevan Davies is correct here in seeing the teaching of two creations underlying this saying.[5] The second creation is the surface world to which we are socialized; it is based on all the arbitrary distinctions of society with their accompanying prejudices: Men are better than women, rich people better than poor people, straight people better than gay people, good-looking people better than ugly people, and so on. This "accepted" world is no better than a corpse. The first creation is the nondualistic realm of the living God whose only time is the Eternal Now and whose only place is Here.

> 61c **Therefore I say that if one is unified one will be filled with light, but if one is divided one will be filled with darkness.**

Dualism is natural to second creation thinking. It is the binary system in which all of our languages are programmed. From the time we are little children, we learn that this is a dog. And that means, of course, that everything else is "not dog." And at the level of second creation, that is true; but at the level of first creation, it is not. You can stand at the beach, seeing the waves rushing to the shore, and name them as they roll toward you. I think I'll call that one "Jane" and that other one "John." But you can also realize that all the waves are water. If we only see reality at the dualistic level, we are in darkness. When we begin to experience the deeper language of unity, we are filled with light.

> 63 **Jesus said: Once there was a rich man who had lots of money, and he said, "I will invest my money so that I can sow, reap, plant, and fill up my silos with crops so that I won't lack anything." So he**

> **thought, but that night he died. He who has ears, let him hear.**

This rich man is an icon in our society today. I remember a student coming back from winter break and telling me that she was very sad at Christmas dinner. When I asked why, she said that her dad (who was a CEO) had made a toast, announcing that the company had made record profits. But then, she went on to say, with a kind of sadness in his voice, he added the comment: "It will really be hard for us to beat this record next year." She realized in that moment that her father was caught. He could never have enough. He had made a god out of what was only meant to be a means to an end. How dramatically the parable ends: "But that night he died."

Practice

Our practice needs to fit each of us the way a glove fits a hand. It needs to be integral and holistic. There have been far too many dualistic spiritualities separating body and soul, so my focus here is our body work. God's Spirit works in our bodiliness, as well as in our thinking, our willing, and our praying. Body work entails any form of awareness that brings us into a deeper and more loving contact with our bodiliness. There are, of course, many classes in yoga available these days, or classes in tai chi, or any number of other Asian disciplines. My own practice is a simple hour at the gym once or twice a week. And then, of course, there is walking, especially if you have the opportunity to walk in a beautiful area, in woods or near a lake.

Whatever physical practice you choose, keep in mind the kind of awareness we spoke of in chapter 1. Feel the life in your body: in your arms and legs, in your belly and back. Feel your feet touching the ground. Be aware of breathing. There are many forms of practice based on breathing. I like to use a phrase that I adopted from Thich Nhat Hanh and modified slightly: "Breathing in I relax my body (inhale); breathing out I smile (exhale). Attentive in the present moment (inhale), I practice here the while (exhale)." Repeating this phrase can meaningfully fill some of the "empty" spots in our day—when we're standing in a checkout line or stopped for a freight train or a red light.

Part of this body work entails becoming aware of every part of our bodily existence. What do we eat and drink? What are the circumstances in which we eat and drink? Is it a matter of wolfing down some processed food while we catch the evening news on the television? Or can we savor a bowl of nourishing soup, a simple piece of cheese, a glass of wine? How well do we sleep? Do we have a partner with whom we can be physically intimate and with whom we can enjoy lovemaking? How much responsibility do we take for our own health? The body is a blessing and we need to cherish it. Practice is integral. It is our whole life. Nothing is left out. The rabbis have given us many blessings; there is even one for our bowel movements. In it we thank God for the body with all of its orifices and all the means by which it is purged of waste and toxins.

How healthy this holism is, compared to the dualistic spiritualities from which so many of us suffer. I recall the chilling movie *The Magdalene Sisters.* In one scene, the Mother Superior chides a young girl for her promiscuity. The girl pleads her innocence, vowing that she has never had sexual relations with a man. "But you thought about it," snaps back the Mother Superior. There was the final proof. She thought about sex. And yet, my good Mother Superior, whence comes that thought about sex? Is it not from the God who made us as sexual beings? No matter how hard you try to block out your body with your black robes, you too are a sexual being with all the longings that make us human. And when we don't recognize the holiness of that sexual desire, we experience the distortions presented in two of the other sisters in that cold and loveless convent.

I have learned much in this regard from my study of Judaism and Islam. I delighted in learning about the Sabbath, how that culminating day of the week celebrates the anticipation of the end times, the fullness of life and love, the time when God is symbolically united again with the *Shekhinah*, the feminine presence of God residing in the world in its experience of exile. So when life partners make love on Friday evening, they are expressing this anticipated union between God and the *Shekhinah*. I was shocked on first hearing this. When have you last heard a Catholic priest encourage his parishioners to make love before coming to Sunday Mass?

There was a day in class during my graduate studies that will long live in my memory. My rabbi teacher was quoting a passage from the Palestinian Talmud reminding us that we will be called to task on Judgment Day for the pleasures of God's world that we failed to enjoy. I raised my hand and asked if perhaps the teacher had wrongly read the passage. He chuckled and told me that I was thinking like a Christian. And I was. I had been reared with a spirituality of holy abstinence in which we got closer to God by getting farther from the world, from matter, from pleasure. Here was a theology of blessed participation in which we meet the Divine by enjoying the beauties and pleasures of life. As the great philosopher and religious teacher Martin Buber pointed out: "The world is not an obstacle on the way to God; it is the way."

Just as we learn about our cultural biases by living in other countries, so do we learn about our religious biases by dialogue with other spiritual traditions. I was having dinner with a close Muslim friend one evening and I remarked that it was difficult for me to think of the prophet Muhammad as a deeply spiritual man, since he maintained to the end of his life such an obvious appreciation for the beauty of his wives and for the joys of sex.

Like my rabbi teacher in the classroom, my Muslim friend said, laughing, "Ron, you are thinking like a Christian again." And it struck me that he was absolutely right. Why should someone highly evolved spiritually not have an interest in sex? And then my friend went on to say that it was difficult for him as a Muslim to trust a spiritual leader who did not have a partner with whom he or she could be sexually intimate.

So as we walk our spiritual paths, we want to remember that we walk with our bodies, as well as with our souls. We need to pay attention to our bodies. They tell us things about ourselves. It is sometimes in a bodily message that we have the first opportunity to learn about something affecting us at a deeper level. I was in the midst of a painful marriage situation when I was found to have an inflamed gall bladder. Being anatomically ignorant, I asked my physician exactly what the problem was. He said that my gall bladder was like a cup that received bile from the liver and that my cup was too full. It was as though lightning had struck me. My cup of bile and bitterness was indeed too full. Within a few months, after counseling efforts failed, I had initiated a process of separation and divorce. So our body is a good teacher and body work is integral to our practice. For the self we are called to become is both whole and holy.

Reflections

1. Do I think of myself as having a body or being a body? In other words, is my body just a temporary embarrassment or is it an integral part of what I am?
2. Do I experience a disconnect between my body and my spiritual life? Does it make sense to chain smoke while discussing consciousness expansion?
3. It's 8 p.m.; where is your mind? It's 8 p.m.; where is your soul? It's 8 p.m.; where is your body? Wouldn't it be nice if they were all together?

4

Religion, Organized and Unorganized

6 His disciples questioned him: Should we fast? In what way should we pray? Should we give to charity? From which foods should we abstain? Jesus responded: Do not lie. If there is something that you hate, do not do it, for everything is revealed beneath heaven. Nothing hidden will fail to be displayed. Nothing covered will remain undisclosed.

FASTING AND DIETARY LAWS, ALMSGIVING, AND PRAYER—THESE ARE central religious practices. They are found among Jews, Christians, Muslims, and peoples not of the Abrahamic traditions. Jesus seems to ignore these standard areas of religious practice. Instead, he tells his disciples not to lie, not to do anything they hate, and to realize that everything will be displayed and disclosed in the light of the divine mystery. Everything "beneath heaven" will be revealed in heaven, in the light of eternity, in the light of ultimate reality.

Why this answer? Because these are standard practices of religion, and religion becomes problematic in certain specific ways. Religion falls prey to certain specific temptations, the greatest of which is hypocrisy. That's why, in telling his disciples not to lie, Jesus lays bare what is most closeted in organized religion: hypocrisy. In telling the disciples not to do what they hate, Jesus is warning them not to follow certain religious observances "to keep up appearances." Finally, in telling his disciples that everything is disclosed to heaven, he is reinforcing this admonition to avoid hypocrisy by reminding them that all duplicity will one day be revealed in the light and truth of the Divine.

Why is hypocrisy such a problem for religious communities? Because shared observances lead to shared expectations; and shared expectations lead to the opportunity to judge others; and being judged by others leads one to do things "to keep up appearances." Having lived in a religious community for many years, I have firsthand knowledge of how this works. We start with a shared set of rules that everyone in the group is expected to observe. In the seminary I entered at seventeen, we rose at 5 a.m., meditated for an hour, went to Mass, maintained silence for most of the day, and went to bed at 9:10 p.m. This meant that if someone slept late, everyone else knew it, especially since we lived in cubicles with curtains, not in private rooms. If someone broke the rule of silence, others knew it. If someone missed Mass, others knew it. This created an environment where everyone knew a great deal about everyone else's practice.

Advent and Lent, the seasons before Christmas and Easter, were times of fasting. There were over two hundred of us and the question of who could fast the most became competitive at times. I remember that a classmate and I would go down to the refectory, eat a quick bowl of cold cereal, and be leaving the refectory while others were still entering it. This made us the gold medalists of fasting. The rule required us to go to breakfast and eat something but it didn't say how much we needed to eat or how long we needed to remain there. Those who dawdled over their food or had second helpings would never make the Fasters' Hall of Fame.

Now once you see how this works, you can understand how it applies to every aspect of religious life, whenever there are shared rules and shared expectations. Is Joe observing the Yom Kippur fast as strictly as Sam? Did Taha see Ahmad end his Ramadan fast before sunset yesterday? Did Mike see Pat eating meat on a Friday of Lent? Did Tyler see Randy drinking a beer at the bar down the road from the

Bible college they both attend? How can such an environment help but lead to hypocrisy? This is why we find Jesus refraining from recommending *rules* of behavior. However, this is not the same thing as refraining from recommending *principles* of behavior.

One can have individual practices that are not part of a rule. No one knows if I have been practicing attention today, if I went to the gym, if I meditated. This means no one can judge my practice. And that's why I'm not as likely to do something I hate in order to keep up appearances. This is the kind of practice Jesus is recommending and it is, therefore, what makes sense for most Thomas Believers. Don't adopt a practice so that everyone knows what you're doing and when you're expected to do it.

But, you may ask, what if a group of us want to meditate together every morning at 6 a.m.? What if some of us want to study a page of Talmud every afternoon at 3 p.m.? What if a few of us want to say the Muslim prayer together every evening? That's fine, but what if it were an opportunity instead of an obligation? I was attending Mass some years ago in Albuquerque, New Mexico, on the Feast of the Assumption of Mary. In his sermon, the priest presiding at the liturgy said, "I think a holy day of obligation is a contradiction in terms. A holy day is a holiday and a holiday is something you *want* to celebrate. This is not a holy day of obligation; this is a holy day of opportunity." I think that comment would make a lot of sense to Thomas Believers. An obligation can be judged by others; opportunity, however, lies beyond such judgment.

Every two years or so, I enjoy spending some time at the monastery of Gethsemani near Bardstown, Kentucky. This is where Thomas Merton, one of my spiritual mentors (not one I knew personally), spent twenty-seven years until his untimely death in 1968. During my many visits, I've come to know some of the monks there. Monastic life used to be rigidly uniform, one of those situations where everyone can judge everyone else. But one of the changes in recent times is that the abbot works with each individual monk in structuring his practice. One monk might sleep in and miss the early morning chanting and another monk might use a Buddhist form of meditation instead of the community prayer. Obviously, this benefits the individual, but, more important, it helps to create an environment where one monk cannot so readily judge another monk's practice. Judgment can never be eliminated completely, especially for people who live in the public eye; but the opportunities for judgment can be decreased and that seems to be the purpose of this teaching.

> **14a Jesus said to them: If you fast you will bring sin to yourselves, and if you pray you will be condemned, and if you give to charity you will damage your spirits.**

This provides a natural complement to saying 6. We are surely not being told that fasting, praying, and almsgiving are sins that damage our spirits. But we are being told that *regulated and required* fasting, praying, and almsgiving readily lead to sin and damage our spirits. Now this obviously contradicts the practices of most organized religions; this, after all, is precisely what makes them organized. To me that is part of the radical character of Thomas Believers. They can enjoy the fellowship of other spiritual adults without a structured religious practice.

This seems like a contradiction. Is the Gospel of Thomas really advocating "unorganized" religion? Quite possibly. And unorganized religion is definitely what I am proposing in this guidebook. We don't need an external agent programming our spiritual lives. Thomas Believers are adults; and real adults (and that certainly doesn't include everyone over twenty-one years of age) don't need an externally imposed regimen. Adults are self-starters, capable of managing their own time and pursuing their own goals.

Since I am still on winter break, there is nothing on my schedule today, except to write this book. I woke up when I woke up. I will eat when I am hungry. I will take a walk when I need a break. I will nap if I am tired. This is completely different from the schedule I followed in the seminary. There every minute of my day was planned, allowing me fifteen minutes of *tempus liberum* (free time) in a day of *ordo regularis* (regular order).

Such a regimen was useful for me when I was seventeen, though I believe that even then it was too much of a good thing. Beginners need structure. When I was learning to dance at the Arthur Murray Dance Studio of my youth, there were patterns on the floor and we looked down at them as we learned to master the steps of the waltz and the fox trot. But when we were finally ready for the sock hop or prom, we no longer needed the patterns on the floor. So many religious folks today have been frozen at an early stage of spiritual development. They have been infantilized. At fifty or sixty years of age they are still asking "Father" what to do. They are still checking the book to see if they're praying at the right time or using the correct words.

I remember an encounter with the mother of a friend of mine. She was a devout Catholic, a woman of sixty-five. She said to me, "Ron, I am really becoming a bad Catholic." "Why is that, Mary?" I asked her. "Because I don't say my prayers anymore." Our ensuing discussion revealed that she had been taught in grade school to say a certain number of prayers by rote each day. But now she was telling me that when she starts to say these prayers, she finds herself just communicating with God; when all is said and done, she hasn't "finished her prayers." I was happy to see this blossoming of the spirit of prayer in this lovely woman but sad to see how little her church had promoted her growth. She was still feeling guilty about not following the patterns on the floor when she danced.

Organized religion will continue to play a necessary role in the formation of many Christians, Jews, Muslims, Buddhists, and the like. But my hunch is that only two kinds of religious institutions will continue to thrive. The first kind will be those providing lifelong infantilism for people who do not want to grow up. The second kind will be those offering people who want to grow up a form of religion beyond spiritual infantilism. Thomas Believers will continue to attract some of the latter, those who are drawn to even more independence in their spiritual lives.

I have worked for many years with a program at Lake Forest College called the Independent Scholar Program. We choose candidates from a pool of applicants at the end of their sophomore year. If accepted into the program, these Independent Scholars pursue an interdisciplinary program for their final two years of college, a program resulting in a thesis. During that time, they can function totally on their own through a series of tutorials and independent research projects. The idea is to pull some of the best students out of the regimen of classes that meet on a regular basis and give them the freedom to operate on their own, free from the normal curricular constraints. Perhaps we can envisage Thomas Believers as a kind of Independent Scholar program in spirituality.

This is my vision of contemporary Thomas Believers. They have no formal community organization. They are free to attend or not to attend religious services they find compatible with their spirituality. Thomas Believers can avail themselves of such communities wherever they live. They can also avoid all community worship, if such worship is not conducive to their spiritual growth. Thomas Believers may choose to form support communities but it is crucial that these be opportunities, not obligations.

A group of Thomas Believers meets regularly at my apartment. We begin with meditation and move to discussing each person's spiritual life and growth. There's no "attendance policy" and one need not feel guilty about deciding to do something else that evening. As some people move away to other cities or develop other interests, other people join the circle. It is a welcoming community, offering no basis for judging others because they fail to follow a prescribed regimen. We do support charitable outreach but there too, no one is under any obligation. The environment is supportive and collegial. This seems to me to be the best way to avoid the spiritual damage that so often accompanies organized religion.

Can this kind of loosely knit spiritual association lead to narcissism? Yes, though that seems no more dangerous than infantilism. Nevertheless, this is something that needs to be addressed.

It is important that Thomas Believers have spiritual directors or that their support communities include peer spiritual direction. It is easy to deceive ourselves and it is, therefore, important for each of us to have someone with whom we can be totally honest about our life and practice. We need sustained contact with people of wisdom and discernment.

What about rituals? If Thomas Believers want to celebrate the birth of a child, a committed relationship, a memorial for a departed friend, they can arrange it in a way that is authentic for themselves and those who choose to join them. Nothing *must* be done but neither must anything helpful be avoided. Trust adults to make adult decisions. One community may use many rituals, while another community may prefer no ritual beyond creating an environment of silence and meditation.

I am reminded of a Taoist story. Someone had died and one of his associates was on the way to the temple for the proper funeral observances. On passing a house where a good friend of the deceased lived, he heard loud laughter and noise. When he entered the house, he found several friends of the deceased sitting on the floor and imbibing freely from large bottles of plum wine. "Why are you sitting here drunk when your friend has died and the funeral services are about to begin? You should be mourning him." The friends responded: "We are mourning him; in fact, you have joined us in the middle of the service."

27a If you do not fast from the world you will not find the Kingdom.

We have spoken of fasting from food, how it might be allowable as a private practice but should be rejected as a common regulation for a community because of the occasion it presents to judge others. The temptation to judge others will inevitably be there but at least we can avoid situations that promote it. But beyond the whole discussion of when or how to fast from food lies a deeper issue. What is it from which we really need to fast? The world.

We have seen this theme in several of the sayings and we cannot stress its importance enough. Most of our behavior is socialized behavior. I remember an occasion when my former wife and I were going on a trip and leaving our children with their grandparents. My son, who was about twelve, came up to me to plead his case. He and his sister didn't really need baby sitters. They could survive at home alone. I asked him what he would do if we did leave him alone. His answer was immediate. "I'd have a toga party." How did that concept get into his twelve-year-old imagination? Had he seen *Animal House* or heard some college-age students talking about such a party?

This led me to the realization that most of the education of our children comes from the media. What they learn in school or hear in church or synagogue forms just a minuscule part of their real education. Hundreds of hours of television lure them into a consumer society, convincing them that earning lots of money is the key to their salvation. It's difficult to know what can really challenge our children to surrender this addiction to "the world." The example of people in their lives who live by different standards is the first and most obvious challenge to worldliness and an invitation to a deeper life. Thomas Believers need to live in such a way that both this challenge and this invitation can be clearly heard.

27b If you do not keep the Sabbath as a Sabbath you will never see the Father.

Although we don't have any immediate context for this saying, the examples we have seen in other sayings help to place it in context. The Sabbath falls into the same category of regular religious observance as fasting, prayer, and almsgiving. Think of the "blue laws" in our history, which were based on the strange notion that designating one day a week in which anything fun was prohibited would constitute a day pleasing to the Lord. The very word *sundae* developed in a context where people couldn't consume alcohol on the Christian Sabbath (i.e., Sunday) so they ate ice cream instead.

What is Jesus thinking about in speaking of keeping the Sabbath "as a Sabbath"? He is going back again to that primordial time before historical time, that mythic state of nondualistic consciousness in which the Sabbath first appears. In the first creation story, God blessed the seventh day and made it holy, "because on it God rested from all the work that he had done in creation" (Genesis 2:3). This demonstrates the holiness both of work and of rest.

Spiritual teachings come in pairs. Work is good; and yet, our society distorts the goodness of work in the lives of so many workaholics. Rest is good; and yet, our society distorts the goodness of rest in the lives of so many "couch potatoes." We always need to seek balance. We should work hard when we work. But we need to respect the holiness of rest, recognizing that the world is sustained by a power far greater than our ego. Such a rest is a true Sabbath.

> **14c For what goes into your mouth will not defile you, but what comes out of your mouth can defile you.**

At a time when dietary practices were a hallmark of religious observance, Jesus turned his hearers' attention to the deeper meaning of defilement. I've been in restaurants where people are eating only kosher food; and yet I've seen some of those same people deal with the wait staff in a patronizing and insensitive manner. I've sat with Catholics observing all the details of a strict Lenten fast and seen some of them verbally abuse their children or their spouses. Jesus always draws our attention to what is of prime importance, helping us to put the lesser things in perspective. He helps us to see "the practice within the practice." A Jewish teaching tells us, "If you are fasting, carry a piece of food with you in your pocket." Why? So that if we get too obsessed with the fasting, we can eat.

Practice

Look at your practice, if you have one, and ask yourself how much you like it. Is it the kind of practice you can do when no one else is watching? Try this little experiment. Decide that you want some spiritual practice in your day and then plan it and engage in it as an adult, doing only those things that make sense to you and seem to promote your awareness and growth. Continue doing this for another day, and then another one. After a week, look back and see how this compares to the kind of week of practice you were used to before this exercise.

Reflections

1. If I have any spiritual practices, do I engage in them only to please someone else? only to keep up appearances? only to be thought well of by others?
2. Do I ever step outside the box of any of the regular practices I was taught? Have I ever invented a ritual? written a hymn? planned a community celebration?
3. Do I engage in a spiritual narcissism—just doing the kinds of things I "feel" like doing? Do I have a spiritual friend to check my practice, to keep me honest?

5

Being a Healing Presence

14b When you go into a region and walk around in the rural areas, whenever people receive you, eat whatever they provide for you, and heal their sick.

ONE NOTICES THE OPEN-ENDEDNESS IN THIS INJUNCTION. THE DISCIPLES are just "walking around" in a rural area. They encounter some people who receive them; presumably, others don't. They are offered food to eat, and at a time when dietary laws were one of the primary norms for judging who was religious and who was not, Jesus is telling them to eat whatever is provided. The one clear command is to be a healing presence.

This saying stands in such sharp contrast to the average proselytizing scenario we have all experienced. There is a knock at the door and when we open the door we find one or two smiling people who are eager to help us. They never ask about the way in which we experience the divine mystery. They have the answer, the right answer, *our* right answer. They know how we should find God better than we ourselves could possibly know. Why is that? Because they have the infallible book—the Bible, the Book of Mormon, or whatever. Or they have the infallible leader or the infallible method of salvation—we just need to accept Jesus or Krishna. There's no reciprocity here. We have no "food" to offer them. They are full, full of themselves, full of ego, full of indoctrination, full of other people's answers.

My favorite Buddhist story is about a great teacher who is invited to a king's court because the king wants to be able to boast of having entertained such a spiritual celebrity. The teacher enters and is invited by the king to perform the tea ceremony. He obliges and is soon pouring tea into the king's cup. But he doesn't stop when the cup is full and the tea begins to overflow onto the fine, lacquered tray and then onto the expensive carpet. "Stop," commands the king. "My cup is full." Bowing, the teacher leaves the court. The full cup can receive no more tea. The "true believer" has no space to learn from others. And without that space to learn, that space to be open to the experience of the other, one can never be a true healer.

There is a beautiful Jewish story about a young man who is deeply attached to his rabbi. He feeds on his every word and spends every waking moment with him. One day he says to the rabbi, "Rabbi, I love you." The rabbi responds, "Ah, you love me, do you? Then tell me where I hurt." The young man, startled by this response, replies: "Rabbi, I have no idea where you hurt." "In that case," the rabbi tells him, "you cannot possibly love me." This is as true of healing as of loving; healing, after all, is a form of loving. We can't love or heal another until we take time to learn where they hurt, to feel the world from their side.

What is healing? It is whatever leads to wholeness and, therefore, it naturally involves many of the practices we have been considering. It entails, for example, a capacity to be present to others. This in turn means that we are present to ourselves. Neither of these qualities can be taken for granted in our society. As a matter of fact, they are more often lacking. Most of us operate at a hectic pace of mindlessness where we are present neither to ourselves nor to others. There have been numerous studies in which chosen researchers move around at cocktail parties, smile at those they meet, and mention that they are dying of cancer. No one hears them. People merely smile, utter a cocktail party cliché ("Aren't these canapés delicious?"), and disappear in the crowd.

Healing involves a form of generosity, a giving of our time to another's hurt. When my mother was dying in the hospital, I noticed the mechanical nature of the procedures employed by many of the medical personnel. The hospital chaplain, however, was a skilled minister who brought true compassion to her ministry; she spent real time with my mother and was with her when she died. There was also an African-American custodian who would come in now and then to empty waste bins and tidy up the room. She would walk over to my mother, take her hand, and ask her with total sincerity, "How are you doing today, sweetie?" My mother would always manage a smile for these two women. They were healing presences in her final days on earth. And they are as rare in hospitals as in any other institutional settings in our culture.

Practice

Is there a set form for healing? There need not be. One can, however, use forms that have been part of healing traditions for centuries. We read, for example, in the Letter of James 5:14–15 that believers can anoint the sick with oil and pray for them. This is the origin of the Christian sacrament of "extreme unction," which is now called "the sacrament of the sick." During my years of clerical ministry, I found this a very beautiful way to bring healing to the sick. I spent the summer after my ordination in a parish and my mornings were filled with visits to hospitals and nursing homes, administering this sacrament to countless people who needed spiritual comfort and healing.

This is something any Thomas Believer can do with any ailing friend for whom this would be appropriate. Create a pleasing environment. Light candles or incense, if these are agreeable to the person who is sick. Then take a small dish of an oil pleasing to you and your ill friend (I prefer eucalyptus) and anoint the person as you pray or sing a message of healing. Remain together in silence, opening yourselves to the healing environment.

There are also ways of praying for the sick when they are at a distance. See the person you are praying for as clearly as you can in your mind's eye. Then raise your right hand, palm outward, and envisage healing energies being transmitted to that person. If you know the place of the pain or disease, imagine the energies touching the body at that point. Some people see the energies as color, especially blue. Meanwhile, place your left hand on your own heart, and feel those same energies and colors healing you.

You might want to use a healing prayer. I learned a beautiful prayer from a Jewish friend of mine who has a healing ministry. "God is my strength; God is my light; God is my life; God is my healing." This prayer also honors the four great archangels: Gabriel, Uriel, Michael, and Raphael, for the roots of their names relate to those divine qualities. You can repeat this prayer together for several minutes, silently praying between the repetitions.

Reflections

1. Am I a healing presence? Or am I so consumed with my own agenda that I have no room for the needs of others?
2. Do I try to hear where others are hurting? Can I read between the lines of what they are saying to me?
3. Have I ever tried some kind of ritual for sending healing to others, whether they were nearby or far away?

6

Peace, Bad and Good

16a Jesus said: People think, perhaps, that I have come to throw peace upon the world. They don't know that I have come to throw disagreement upon the world, and fire, and sword, and struggle.

16b [For] there will be five in one house. Three will oppose two. Two will oppose three. The father will oppose his son and the son oppose his father. And they will stand up and they will be alone [*monachos*].

THERE IS BOTH BAD AND GOOD PEACE. PEACE IS FINE WHEN IT IS THE FRUIT of justice, but it is not fine when it condones injustice. As the Qur'an states: "And fight in God's cause against those who wage war against you, but do not commit aggression—for verily, God does not love aggressors … and drive them away from wherever they drove you away—for oppression is even worse than killing" (The Cow: 190–191).[6] If armed resistance is the only way to protect the innocent, then it may be necessary in this unevolved world in which we live. One may be able to pursue justice without any use of force, but the use of force in pursuing justice is better than simply accepting an unjust situation. In other words, it is justice, not the absence of force, that is the absolute in conduct.

The saying goes on to talk about families. As we have seen in an earlier saying, families can be stifling ego cocoons. The Thomas Believer is called to be *monachos*, alone. This is the same word used for a monastic. Should we all be monastics? If this means men and women who live in cells, praying all night, and fasting on bread and water, no. But if this means people who have learned to live alone as adults, then, yes, we are all called to be monastics.

What about relationships? Friendships? Sexual unions? We have to remember that many of these are forms of codependence. A healthy relationship, friendship, or sexual union needs people who can stand alone. Students will sometimes come to me and say of their significant other, "I can't live without her." My response is always, "Then you're not ready to live with her." We're only ready to live with people when we know we can live without them. Run as quickly as you can from people who want to make you happy. If you let them make you happy, then they can make you unhappy, and you have become a puppet to their whims. Find happiness in yourself and then share it with others who find happiness in themselves; such a coming together is a beautiful celebration. Just as adults are so rare in our world, so too are adult relationships.

21a Mary asked Jesus: Who are your disciples like? He replied: They are like little children in a field that does not belong to them. When the field's owners come they will say: "Give our field back." They will strip naked in the owners' presence and give it back, returning their field to them.

Jesus's disciples are depicted as being in a field that does not belong to them. Given children and a field, we can presume they are playing. I remember one of the old monks at Gethsemani saying one day that the monastic life is playful. The monks meet seven times a day to sing praises to God; they eat a little, work a little, nap a little. But they don't do anything that "the world" considers to be serious business. This means that they have learned to take the world lightly. In this sense, all Thomas Believers should play in the field of the world. And true play is an expression of true peace.

We also note in saying 21a that the field does not belong to the children. They are passersby, not investing themselves in the transient show of this world. When they are asked to give the field back, they go a step further and leave not only the field but their clothes. They want to be encumbered by nothing. I have a special friend and when I'm at his apartment, I never say that I like anything there. I have learned from experience that as soon as I say that, he immediately gives me the object I admire. He truly lives lightly in this world, an important quality of a Thomas Believer.

This saying gives us an image of Eden consciousness: Adam and Eve when they were still naked but without shame or fear. They knew themselves to be called "to serve and preserve the garden Earth" (Genesis 2:15) but they understood themselves as the gardeners, not as the owners of the garden. This was a mythic time before sin, before alienation, before the objectification of people and nature. This is where Thomas Believers should live. This is the consciousness they should inhabit.

21b Therefore I say: If a householder knows a thief is coming, he will keep watch and not let him break into his house (of his kingdom) and steal his goods.

21c You must keep watch against the world, preparing yourselves with power so that thieves will not find any way to come upon you.

The image of the "thief in the night" has entered into our common language. The phrase appears in the books of the Christian Testament but with a different meaning: there it refers to Jesus's return. This is a strained and unnatural metaphor. Why compare Jesus to a thief? This is an excellent example of how the original stories of Jesus were sometimes given a different spin to suit the beliefs of a later age. As mainstream Christians became more and more preoccupied with an anticipated future, the present struggle with the socialized world seemed less important. So the very useful and timely admonition of Jesus to be alert to the "world" that would rob us of our true peace becomes a meaningless warning to watch out for the end of the world and the return of Jesus, a totally unrealistic future-oriented scenario.

I remember an occasion when the Dalai Lama was being interviewed and the journalist asked him if he hated the Chinese. The Dalai Lama smiled that wonderful smile of his and said that the Chinese had already taken a great deal from the people of Tibet but if he hated the Chinese, then he would be letting them take his most prized possession, his own peace. Bitterness, rancor, greed, jealousy—how many thieves there are out there who would rob us of peace.

Practice

Conflict in life is inevitable but we can be more or less skilled in our modes of conflict resolution. For a wonderful book on both understanding and developing the skill of nonviolent conflict resolution, I recommend Michael Nagler's *Is There No Other Way?: The Search for a Nonviolent Future.*[7] He makes a convincing argument that, in the long run, and sometimes in the short run too, nonviolent action is what works.

I was dean of students at Lake Forest College for eight years and I learned a lot about conflict resolution. There were roommate conflicts, conflicts between the Greeks and the Independents, conflicts between the conservatives and the liberals, conflicts between races, ethnic groups, even geographical parts of the country. I always tried to lead with the educational model. What do the two conflicting parties have in common? When you persist in asking this question, you will always find something.

Then move to dialogue and eventually to resolution, or at least to an agreement to disagree peacefully.

A good part of this skill has to do with careful listening. In teaching dialogue, I will often require the person speaking to hold a pencil. If another person wants to speak, she does not get the pencil until repeating, to the first person's satisfaction, a synopsis of what that person has said. I've done these exercises over some thirty years now and have discovered that in about 45 percent of the cases, the speaker does not feel adequately understood by the summary expressed by the person wanting to respond. Think what that means for all the conversations going on in the workplace and home where these rules are not being followed.

Reflections

1. Do I see the difference between good and bad peace, between a peace that merely masks reality's wounds and one that heals them?
2. Do I seek conflict resolution respecting all the parties and viewpoints involved, or do I just try to steamroll over everyone else with my own perspective? Do I have a reputation for really hearing people?
3. Do I play fair? in my workplace? in the intimacy of my bedroom? at the dinner table?

7

Childlike, Not Childish

22a Jesus saw infants being suckled. He said to his disciples: These infants taking milk are like those who enter the Kingdom.

So often Jesus sees in infants and little children the perfect models of the Eden consciousness. These infants are nursing at their mothers' breasts. They do not yet really understand their reality as separate from that of their mothers. How like the greatest mystics and saints. All their food comes from the Divine Mother and they do not operate out of dualistic consciousness; they do not see themselves as separate from the God who nurtures them, the God who is as close as the mother's breast, the God who is their own deepest reality. This is the positive side of being childlike, a quality of true adults. Being childish or infantile, however, is what characterizes those who are not spiritually mature.

22b His disciples asked him: If we are infants will we enter the Kingdom? Jesus responded: When you make the two into one, and when you make the inside like the outside and the outside like the inside, and the upper like the lower, and thus make the male and the female the same, so that

> **the male isn't male and the female isn't female. When you make an eye to replace an eye, and a hand to replace a hand, and a foot to replace a foot, and an image to replace an image, then you will enter the Kingdom.**

Davies insightfully points out that this verse takes us back to the first days of creation.[8] The human being was made in the image and likeness of God (Genesis 1:27). Only later in the story (Genesis 2:21–22) will one side (another possible translation of the word we usually translate as rib) of that human being become female and one side male. There are many rabbinic commentaries about the androgynous character of the human being before this sexual differentiation took place.

The key to the meaning of saying 22b lies in the last phrase, where Jesus speaks of an image replacing an image. The image of men and women as competitors for power, one being dominated by the other, one being a sex object for the other—all of this belongs to the superficial world that does not embody God's reign. We must return to the original androgynous image, our shared humanness, to live together as a community manifesting God's reign. It is in this sense that one image replaces another.

We're not told whether the hearers of this teaching understood this as a call to celibacy. If so, we would then see the transition from *monachos* as the one who is alone to the monastic, the man and woman who lives alone, without an intimate other, without a sexual partner. I don't think one has to pursue the insight in that direction. We do have to be alone, as we learned in the last saying. And we do have to see and act in the world with an awareness of the divine image shared by men and women. In other words, Thomas Believers must be totally egalitarian in terms of any gender issues. But I don't think that prohibits sexual partnerships between men and women, women and women, or men and men. These partnerships must be between equals, however, and not conform to the dominance patterns of the larger society.

This equality of gender accounts for some of the hostility shown toward Thomas Believers by the larger institutions, which tend to be deeply entrenched in patriarchy. Some people bemoan the sensationalism of Dan Brown's *The Da Vinci Code*, and it does contain a great number of factual errors. Nevertheless, it has occasioned much fruitful discussion and it has led people to the solid work being done by scholars like Elaine Pagels and Karen King.[9] Although I maintain a healthy skepticism toward most conspiracy theories, there was without question a conspiracy in the patriarchal Church to marginalize women and to ignore the emancipating stance toward women taken by Jesus.

This oppression of women continues to be one of the major injustices within many of the organized Christian bodies, especially the Eastern Orthodox and Roman Catholic communities. Not only does this do harm to women, but it does harm to the whole community by making all of that talent unavailable. I dined recently with two women, both of whom had served the Catholic Church for twenty years as members of religious communities, as sisters. One is now an Episcopal priest and one is the president of a Unitarian church. The suppression of women in some Christian churches continues to enrich other more welcoming communities.

The injustice of patriarchy is not, of course, limited to Christians. A friend of mine likes to quip with women who admire the Dalai Lama that they would probably not enjoy life as a Tibetan Buddhist nun. The lives of Jewish women are often similarly circumscribed, especially in Orthodox Judaism, as are those of many Muslim women, Hindu women, and women in virtually every religious tradition. It's ironic that religions are often more in agreement in the way they sin than in the way they practice virtue.

25 Jesus said: Love your brother as your own soul.
Protect him as you protect the pupil of your eye.

A Thomas Believer must be rooted in love and Jesus's image here provides us with a striking metaphor for that love. How quickly our hand moves to protect our face if something is coming toward our eyes. If we had that same instinct for our fellow human beings, we would be living in a paradisiacal world. That's precisely the world Jesus calls us to create and, consequently, the kind of communities we are called to create as well. When we see people being denied justice because of their race, religion, gender, sexual orientation, or any other aspect of their humanness, we must react as promptly as if our own life were being attacked.

> **26 Jesus said: You see the splinter in your brother's eye, but you do not see the log that is in your own eye. Remove the log from your own eye, and then you can clearly see to remove the splinter from your brother's eye.**

If saying 25 gives us the positive side of a truth about loving others, then saying 26 gives us the negative side of that same love, the avoidance of a judgmental attitude. We are quick to sharply criticize the behavior of others while often ignoring our own inappropriate behavior. I found myself annoyed the other day at a driver on a cell phone who was swerving around in traffic, obviously distracted by the conversation. And then I remembered times when I was dialing a number on my cell phone and not paying sufficient attention to my own driving. Why am I so harsh in criticizing others and so lax in self-criticism? A good community is one where we all are more attentive to our own failings than to those of others.

Practice

The spontaneous love and generosity so often shown by a child exemplifies a wonderful practice. And yet, deeds of loving-kindness are dangerous if performed without awareness. People can be helped only by those who know them, those who are aware of who they are and what they are feeling at a given time. How often do we find ourselves running away from someone trying to be nice to us? Their mistake lies in their effort to do something for us without first being aware of where we are in our life at that point. You may think you are doing friends a favor by trying to draw them into conversation, but it may be a time when they need some silence. Without awareness, efforts at kindness often prove most unkind.

So this practice of deeds of loving-kindness embraces some of the earlier lessons we have grasped. We must, of course, be attentive, knowing ourselves and where we are in the moment. We must be open to others, really hearing what they are saying, as well as what they are not saying. We must try to feel the situation from the other side, walking as much as possible in the shoes of the neighbor who meets us. We must try to put aside the grid of the socialized world that distorts our vision so that we see this person as the wrong color, belonging to the wrong religion, having the wrong sexual orientation, the wrong accent, the wrong socioeconomic status, and the like.

The more we are able to look beyond these things, the more we are able to reach out to the other with sincere kindness. Words of kindness, gestures of kindness, deeds of kindness—they will flow naturally, spontaneously, without preparation or reflection. If we have the openness of the child, we can respond with the guileless innocence of the child. We won't be giving with a hook, in order to win thanks or recognition. We won't be giving to fulfill a rule or requirement. Our kindness and our love will be true. Long ago Thomas Aquinas said that to love is to will the good of the other, and that is what we will try to do in every encounter of our life.

We read in the Talmud that the world rests on three things: study of Torah, worship, and deeds of loving-kindness.[10] We don't have to look far to find opportunities to practice either love or kindness. In a world where our interactions are increasingly defined by cruelty at worst and indifference at best, compassion is a rare commodity. All the more reason to practice it.

Many of us drive on today's congested streets and there is no better place to begin. When I drive in traffic, I'm always aware of how limited I am in my own spiritual progress. We are challenged to substitute road kindness for road rage. "Why are we on the road?" I ask my students. "To get where we're going as quickly as possible," they respond. But a Buddhist article I read suggested that we are on the road to protect the lives of all sentient beings. Does that change our perspective? Very much so. In every situation, we can view our conduct on the road as geared to protecting all the lives that cross our path. This makes driving a different experience, one of compassion rather than competition.

"What's the difference between a tour and a trip?" I ask my students. They answer: "On a trip, you're trying to get someplace, reach a goal; on a tour, on the other hand, you're just looking around and enjoying yourself." Why not make every trip a tour? Again, when we change our mind, we change our experience. On a tour, we are in the here and now. Look at that field. Look at those flowers. People are much nicer when they're on a tour than when they're on a trip. We'll be showing a great deal of compassion to our fellow beings if we try always to be on a tour when we travel.

We can carry this practice of deeds of loving-kindness over to all the anonymous people who cross our paths. The folks at the checkout counter, the wait staff, people asking for handouts on the street, the custodians in our buildings—we can make it a point to look at them and to speak kindly to them. This applies to disfigured people, those with disabilities, or the person at work whom no one likes. Bring kindness and a smile to each of these people. Our efforts won't always be acknowledged but we need to make them nonetheless.

Our practice is based on discerning God's image and likeness in every human being we encounter and ultimately in every sentient being as well. Every time we do this, we are closer to becoming Jesus's twin, for this was his hallmark. Surely those who were met by Jesus—whether they were prostitutes, hated tax collectors, or lepers—felt his loving gaze, an embracing presence revealing to them their innermost identity as icons of God, imprinted with God's sign and seal. It no longer made a difference how they were judged by society.

Each time we act in this way, each time we are attentive in this way, each time we pray in this way, we are softening our own heart chakras, causing that creaky wheel to rotate a bit more easily. There is so much of Jesus that we can incorporate in our own lives: the joy with which he drank in the wonder and beauty of his heavenly Parent's world, the kindness in his eyes when he looked at those in need, the healing presence he brought to everyone he met, the love in his heart when he tried to help people open up to the immensity of God's love. It is a lifetime practice to become Jesus's twin. And yet, I find Jesus's twins among so many people I meet—Jews and Christians, Muslims and Buddhists, atheists and agnostics.

Reflections

1. Do I ever find myself giving to others from my point of view rather than from theirs?
2. Do I ever find myself being kind to others so that they will do something for me in return?
3. Can I imagine myself encountering others the way Moses or Muhammad, Jesus or the Buddha would?

8

Daring to Be a City on a Hill

32 Jesus said: A city built and fortified atop a tall hill cannot be taken, nor can it be hidden.

CHAKRAS ARE AN ANCIENT HINDU PARADIGM FOR UNDERSTANDING spiritual growth. The chakras are understood as centers of energy and each one represents a form of energy activated—or turning—at a certain point in our personal growth. The first chakra is at the base of the spine; this chakra, as well as the next two (at the genital and visceral levels), operates in virtually everyone. The fourth chakra, the heart chakra, starts to turn when a person is capable of altruism, feeling things from the other side. The fifth chakra, in the throat area, signals an openness to intuition and psychic awareness. The sixth chakra, the middle eye, is the seat of wisdom. The seventh and final chakra, the crown chakra, opens up to bliss and joy. The fully energized or evolved person is one whose every chakra is turning.

Jesus is a master of metaphor. How vivid a picture he gives us of a fortified city on a distant hill. How is this like the Thomas Believer? The tall hill represents a higher consciousness, the crown consciousness of the seventh chakra, the place of bliss and joy. Such a consciousness is fortified with the virtues we have seen in these teachings: trust in God, humility, love of neighbor, healing and helping others, giving generously to all, living lightly in the world, balancing work and rest. How can one conquer such a person? And, more important, how can one hide such a person?

33a Jesus said: What you hear in your ears preach from your housetops.

Thomas Believers are not called to live in narcissistic isolation. These teachings are not for mere personal enrichment. There is a "good news" (gospel) to share. The message is to be preached "from your housetops." I understand this as preaching from our higher consciousness, a kind of preaching desperately needed today. So much of what is heard today in church pulpits and television pulpits alike comes from such an unevolved consciousness: calling people sinners and threatening them with hell, denouncing people of other spiritual traditions, urging people to support the preacher's portfolio.

One thinks of the faithful Catholics who have been so generous in putting hard-earned money in the Sunday collections. Now, because of the stubbornness with which Church authority clings to an unrealistic rule of celibacy, millions of dollars are being paid out to try to clean up the mess created by clerical hypocrisy, dishonesty, and abuse of children. What the Church is preaching by this conduct is clearly not a message from the housetops, not a word coming from higher consciousness, and certainly not good news.

33b For nobody lights a lamp and puts it underneath a bushel basket or in a hidden place. Rather, it is placed on a lamp stand so that all who go in and out may see the light.

Light is connected with the sixth chakra, the eye of wisdom. In many traditions, individuals manifesting this wisdom are depicted with light around their heads (halos) or emanating from the center of their foreheads. I doubt that this kind of convergence of spiritual witness from differing traditions is accidental; it stems from a common experience. Our society desperately needs wisdom and this is a quality very different from intelligence. One can know a great deal in a field of specialization and still be what Germans call a *Fachidiot,* one who knows things only within his academic discipline. Wisdom, on the other hand, is a coordinating vision, seeing means in terms of an end, pieces in terms of a whole. Such wisdom, when we are fortunate enough to find it, needs to be placed on a lamp stand to illuminate life as far as possible.

39b You should be as clever as snakes and as innocent as doves.

There is nothing spiritual in the cultivation of stupidity. I remember a demanding Greek teacher telling us one day in class, "Gentlemen, you will all die ignorant; but with a certain amount of effort, you need not die pathetically ignorant." Those words have always consoled me. I will die ignorant. That's a given. But if I work very hard, I need not die pathetically ignorant. It is good then to be as clever as snakes, those ancient symbols of wisdom and cleverness in the Middle East.

But being clever isn't enough. Spiritual wisdom often comes in pairs of insight or understanding. As a Jesuit, I was taught that having only holiness or only intelligence is like trying to walk on one leg. Most Jesuits receive doctorates in their chosen field of interest. But they are also trained to be holy, to embody the spirituality contained in *The Spiritual Exercises of St. Ignatius.* Thomas Believers, too, should walk on two legs. An integral practice includes formation of the mind and of the soul. Just as we stretch our minds in study, so too should we stretch our souls in prayer and meditation.

A dove brought a freshly plucked olive leaf to Noah in his ark, giving him hope that the flood waters had subsided and dry land had appeared (Genesis 8:11). The Holy Spirit descended on Jesus like a dove when John the Baptist plunged Jesus into the waters of the Jordan (Mark 1:10). A dove means innocence and hope, gentleness and beauty. This innocence is not ignorance, however. It is the wisdom that comes from attaining a higher consciousness, one where reason reaches its limit and allows itself to be carried beyond reason to what is mystery. This innocence of deep spirituality is completely compatible with intelligence and wisdom.

49 Jesus said: Blessed are the single ones and the chosen ones, for you will find the Kingdom. Because you emerged from it you will return to it.

We find here once more the theme of the *monachos*, the one who is alone, the single one. We come from God's reign where God is One and we return to God's reign where God is One. We come from a unity consciousness, the Eden consciousness of the first creation. It is from there that we enter the world of the second creation, the world of duality and alienation. Through spiritual practice, we return again to the world of unity consciousness. It is for this path that we have been chosen.

50a Jesus said, If they ask you, "Where are you from?" reply to them, "We have come from the place where light is produced from itself. It came and revealed itself in their image."

50b If they ask you, "Are you it?" reply to them, "We are his Sons. We are chosen ones of the living Father."

We find here again the image of light. Light is the first creation, as well as creation's source; light is our personal goal as Thomas Believers; light is creation's goal as well. We have indeed come from the place where light is produced from itself. Created light, even that of the first creation, is manifested light. God's intrinsic light is the unmanifested light, the source, the Father/Mother God. It is this light that is the source of our deepest reality, our imaging of God. Are we the light? Not in its unmanifest form. We are the children of light, the ones chosen to be light-filled by the source, "the living Father."

50c If they ask you, "What is the sign within you of your Father?" reply to them, "It is movement. It is rest."

What is the sign that reveals our divine source? We find another example here of the pairing of spiritual truths. The sign is movement and rest. Movement is our work in the world; rest is our mystical prayer. It is only together that they constitute the sign that God's reign is within us. If we are only movement, we fall prey to activism; if we are only rest, we fall prey to quietism, the heresy of waiting for God to do everything. The rhythm of prayer and work in our lives is the revelation of God. Thomas Believers are Jesus's twins in being examples both of works (teaching, healing, proclaiming good news) and of rest (God-centeredness, presence, peace).

Practice

We saw that the hill can be understood as higher consciousness. Daring to be a city on a hill means daring to act from a higher consciousness. How do we do that? It's not something we do by straining but by relaxing. Lower levels of consciousness are restrictive; higher levels of consciousness are expansive. So when we're in a situation, it helps to take a few deep breaths. Try to ease into a higher level of consciousness. If you are feeling impulsive, try to be rational. If you are merely rational, try to be intuitive. If you are only intuitive, try to be aware with a unity consciousness, a mystical consciousness.

Think of the people who embody higher consciousness for you. Jesus or the Buddha, Muhammad or Mary, the Dalai Lama or Dorothy Day. Think of a difficult situation you are in and try to imagine walking around inside their body, thinking their thoughts, feeling their feelings, acting from their consciousness in grappling with the people or problems with which you find yourself contending. Then return to yourself and enter the situation, daring to be the city on a hill.

Reflections

1. Do I believe that "the Buddha nature" or "Christ consciousness" is available to ordinary people like me?
2. Can I occasionally experience this shift of consciousness in myself, this way in which I can "change my mind" about how I'm viewing someone or some situation?
3. If so, then how can I enable that to happen more often? Does it mean being more relaxed and reflective in the moment, more open and attentive?

9

Becoming Totally Receptive

53 His disciples asked him: Is circumcision useful or not? He replied: If it were useful, then they would be born already circumcised. On the other hand, true circumcision in the spirit is entirely beneficial.

THIS IS THE SAME KIND OF QUESTION ASKED ABOUT ALMSGIVING, FASTING, prayer, and Sabbath observance. If a woman can be identified by mere external performance, how deep can such an identification be? If a man's spirituality can be judged by his penis, how profound can such a judgment be? If the physical condition of the penis were the true sign of a God-centered man, then a loving God would have created all men with a penis already circumcised. These external signs have validity only if they reflect something more of our essence, something "in the spirit." What is our true receptivity to the divine life in each of us?

54 Jesus said: Blessed are the poor, for yours is the Kingdom of Heaven.

The community of Thomas Believers is called to be poor. But poverty isn't only a matter of what's in our pocketbooks. It's also what's in our hearts. Perhaps that's why Matthew amends the teaching to say: "Blessed are the poor in spirit" (Matthew 5:3). Matthew was probably himself a Jewish scribe who joined the Jesus movement; perhaps he had been a teacher. His use of his sources often shows an interest in making things clear. Poverty is a quality of spirit, just like circumcision. It means living from the Divine Source, like the infants nursing at their mothers' breasts whom Jesus praised. This poverty is the greatest richness.

62b Do not let your left hand know what your right hand is doing.

The biblical injunction not to harvest your fields too carefully reflects a form of charity in which the poor can come to the fields when the workers have gone home and they can gather for themselves whatever is left. The owner is already home; he is not standing around to dole out the grain or fruit to the grateful poor. The more carelessly you harvest, the more generous you are. Anonymity characterizes this high form of charity. Jesus pushes this truth to its hyperbolic conclusion. It's better if not even your left hand knows when the right hand is making a gift to the poor.

69b Blessed are those who are hungry in order to fill the bellies of the needy.

The canonical gospels contain a form of this teaching. In Matthew 5:6 we are told that those who hunger and thirst for God-centeredness are blessed. And in Luke 6:21 we read: "Blessed are you who go hungry; you will be satisfied." But saying 69b has a different twist. These aren't people who are hungry simply because of external circumstances, nor are they hungry in a spiritual sense. They are literally hungry because they are giving everything to feed people even poorer than themselves.

In Jesus's world, about 93 percent of the people were dirt-poor peasants. The Roman Empire, after all, like every empire, needed its sweatshops in every country it conquered. But because some of the building projects at that time displaced peasants from their ancestral lands, a population of destitute and homeless people was created. Jesus urges the poor to take care of the destitute. The poor in saying 69b are poor precisely because they are helping these destitute and homeless people. What does this imply for Thomas Believers today?

> **89 Jesus said: Why wash the outside of the cup? Don't you know that the one who made the inside also made the outside?**

All that can ever be prescribed is external behavior. But judging externals never penetrates to the depths of the heart. It would be silly to wash the outside of the cups you're using to serve your guests but leave the inside of the cups dirty. Is it any less silly to set up an array of rules and regulations for external behavior? Bring your body to church on Sunday. Don't put meat in your stomach on the Fridays of Lent. Cut the foreskin of your penis. Separate meat foods and dairy foods. But when all of this is accomplished, do we know anything at all about what's going on in a person's soul? Maybe that's the place to begin cleaning things up.

> **90 Jesus said: Come to me. My yoke is easy. My mastery is gentle, and you will find rest for yourselves.**

It had long been a Jewish metaphor to speak of Torah observance as a yoke. It has the same root as the word *yoga,* a practice attaching someone to the Divine, just as a yoke attaches one animal to another. But why is Jesus's yoke easy? It seems to be the most difficult yoke of all, since it demands not only external conformity to a set of rules but the deepest dedication of the heart.

Jesus's yoke is easy because it reveals our true nature; it describes the natural flow of our being; it calls us to our deepest essence. It doesn't ask us to lie or to pretend to be something that we aren't or to do things that we hate. It calls us to life, abundant life, the deepest and most honest expression of our being. To avoid Jesus's yoke is to live with distraction and denial, with dishonesty and duplicity. Is that easy? Not really. We do that at a cost. To accept Jesus's yoke is to allow ourselves to become what we have always wanted to be in our most innermost thoughts and aspirations. This means achieving "rest," the deep peace flowing from a life of integrity and truth. This is why Jesus's yoke has nothing to do with joining a particular religious organization but everything to do with becoming Jesus's twin by becoming a spiritual adult.

Practice

The practice I want to introduce at this point is generosity, but, ironically, being able to receive must precede being able to give. And we need to have space in ourselves to appreciate our need to give to others. Being "poor" and "hungry" in the sayings above are examples of having space. Space is what allows us to receive. And we must first realize how much we are receiving before we can grasp the depth of giving required of us. So begin by becoming aware of what you receive: the gift of life each morning, hot running water from the shower faucet, cereal and coffee, the smile of a loved one, and so on through each day. We are major debtors to this universe. And it is only when we grasp this that we can see how natural it is for us to give in return.

We must give generously of our material resources, of our time, and of our talents. There is a convergence here of biblical and Qur'anic teaching. The wealth tax (*Zakat*) is one of the Five Pillars of Islam. A certain amount (normally 2.5 percent) of whatever we have is owed to the poor. But Muslims are enjoined to give beyond what is required by *Zakat*; this further generosity is *Sadaqah*. In page after page of the Qur'an, we are encouraged to generosity. "O you who have attained to faith! Spend on others out of the good things which you may have acquired, and out of that which We bring forth for you from the earth ... " (The Law: 267). There is also a story attributed to Muhammad: "Every morning when people wake up, two angels descend from the heavens. One of them will say, 'Lord! Replace the wealth of a charitable spender.' And the other will say, 'Lord! Diminish the wealth of a stingy person who withholds his wealth from the needy.'"[11]

A Muslim student recently asked to take me out to dinner when he celebrated his birthday. As we were enjoying our meal together, he told me that in his religion, you give to others when it's your birthday. It's such a strange reversal of our American "birthday present" mentality. He said that a Muslim friend ran up to him and said, "What are you giving me for your birthday?" Maybe we should all be "small-*m* muslims" in this regard. Maybe every happy occasion of our life should be a sign for us to give to others.

The Jewish tradition is filled with this same message. The call to take care of widows and orphans cries out from every page of the Hebrew Bible. Jeremiah is told to bring words of condemnation to the house of Jacob. Why? "They know no limits in deeds of wickedness; they do not judge with justice the cause of the orphan, to make it prosper, and they do not defend the right of the needy" (Jeremiah 5:28). And when Isaiah proclaims the true fast God asks of us, it is not refraining from certain foods, but participating in God's cause of justice: "Is the true fast not to share your bread with the hungry and to bring the homeless poor into your house?" (Isaiah 58:7). Rabbi Yose ben Yochanan of Jerusalem told his disciples to "treat the poor as family."[12]

Obviously, we have to pay our bills first and make efforts to maintain our own subsistence, but beyond that we can try to give as much as we can to others. In saying 95 of the Gospel of Thomas we are told: "If you have some money, don't lend it out at interest but give it to someone who will not return it to you." It's better not to set up criteria of deserving and undeserving poor. If the homeless man you give the dollar to uses it for cheap wine rather than food, so what? Research shows that college students spend more for alcohol than for books and well-dressed suburbanites put a great deal of their income into their cocktail and wine glasses. Look at the person in need, trying to recognize the divine image; then give the dollar, and bless that person in your heart. Nothing belongs to us or is ultimately owned by us. We are stewards of the goods of this world. That's why we need to move lightly and generously through the world.

The generosity practiced by individuals can also be incorporated into communities. I recently spoke at a Quaker meeting that is actively promoting fair trade products. Most church, synagogue, and mosque communities have committees involved in deeds of generosity to the poor. If you meet regularly with a meditation group or any other kind of support community for spiritual growth, have a box where people can make a donation when they enter, whatever each person is able to give, and then give that money to aid others in need. Make giving a regular practice. On your birthday, give to the poor. When you're happy, give to the poor. When you're sad, give to the poor. A Thomas Believer is exhorted to let generosity become as natural as breathing.

Reflections

1. Can I take a few minutes right now to make a list of at least some of the countless things I have been given today?
2. Can I understand why taking things for granted, or, even worse, always complaining, is the opposite posture to the gratitude that is so central to any spiritual path?
3. Can I think ahead to what's left of my day today or to my day tomorrow and imagine ways that I can be more generous?

10

Now/Here or Nowhere

EVERYTHING DESCRIBED BY THE METAPHORIC LANGUAGE OF MYSTICAL religion is here and now. And when we put "now" and "here" together, we get "nowhere." The mysteries of religion are nowhere, that is, they are not space and time realities. The greatest challenge in entering the context of this entire discourse lies in disabusing ourselves of this spatial and temporal orientation. Every text must be interpreted in the here and now, because this is the only reality. The past is memory and the future is hope, but the present is everything real.

So when you're asked what God did before God created the world, just smile. And when you're asked what life will be like after we die, just smile. And when all the questions have been asked and you have smiled a basketful of smiles, then ask your interlocutor: "Where are you here and now?" That's where God is, and Jesus, and the Buddha, and Moses, and Muhammad, and the Holy Spirit, and God's Kingdom, and yourself, and your community, and your past, and your future. If the Thomas Believer has a mission, it is to invite everyone she meets to this holy place and time we call "nowhere."

> **30 Jesus said: Where there are three Gods they are Gods. Where there are two or one, I am with him.**

This is one of the only sayings that talks directly about God, and it is one of the most difficult to decipher. Saying 30 revolves around the numbers one, two, and three. Who is the *they* in the first sentence? If it refers to the three gods, it seems to say very little: three gods are gods. Or does it mean that where there are three gods, there is polytheism, the theology embraced by the Roman Empire but rejected by the community of Israel?

It's difficult to read these words without thinking about the later trinitarian theology that develops in Christianity. The average Christian is more than likely a tritheist, that is, someone who believes in three gods. In other words, most Christians pray to Father, Son, and Spirit just as if they were three different people they knew: their mother, their brother, and their next-door neighbor. Is it possible that the source of saying 30, presuming that it is not Jesus himself, saw this incipient trinitarianism in the theology of Paul or in other early Christian writings?

Because the Father, Son, and Spirit function as three distinct personalities for most Christians, many Jewish and Muslim theologians, not to mention Unitarians, have problems understanding the Christian claim to be monotheistic. Saying 30 encourages us to cleanse our faith of any latent polytheism and assert quite clearly that divine mystery is one. Jews pray: Hear, O Israel, the Lord our God, the Lord is one. Muslims proclaim: There is no God but God. Hindus remind us: God is one but known by many names.

The Latin word *persona*, as well as its earlier Greek counterpart, *prosopon*, does not refer to personalities. A *prosopon* ("in front of the face") was originally an actor's mask, just as a *persona* ("sound through") was the mouthpiece through which the actor projected his voice. As theological language moved from Greek to Latin to the various languages of Europe, the "three persons" became increasingly "three personalities" in the day-to-day understanding of most Christians.

And yet, Father, Son, and Spirit are not three gods but three ways in which Christians experience the divine mystery—namely, in the mystery of ongoing creation, in what is revealed as God's Word, and in the movement of God's Spirit in the world. These are three relationships in which the Divine is known, not three divine beings. Just as someone can be a son to his father, a brother to his sister, and a father to his son, so too can God be experienced by Christians in a threefold manner.

The second sentence of saying 30 is even more difficult. *Where there are two* might refer to a level of spirituality where a person feels very close to God and yet understands God as the "wholly other one." This person and God would then be two and Jesus would be with them, in that case, as a third. *Or one* might suggest a higher form of spirituality in which the difference between the person and God has disappeared altogether, so that there is only one. In that case, too, Jesus would be with them, and presumably all three would be one at a higher level of nondualistic consciousness.

This denial of any ultimate duality is central to these teachings. This truth is beautifully expressed in a story by the thirteenth-century Sufi mystic Rumi. Someone comes to the door of his friend and knocks. The person inside asks who is there and the person outside identifies himself: "It is I." His friend inside tells him to go away because there is no room for him. Years later, the friend returns and again knocks on the door. Again he is asked to identify himself. This time he replies: "It is you." And at that point the door is opened. Only identity with the divinity within opens the door of unity consciousness.[13]

> **59 Jesus said: Look at the living one while you live, for if you die and then try to see him you will not be able to do so.**

Many people put off spiritual practice "for the next life." They feel that they are busy now with more important things. Furthermore, our popular culture and its values make the whole world of spirituality seem irrelevant. Ours is a materialistic society, focusing on money and our consumer status. Our culture is one of distraction and denial. We are constantly lured away from the silence and solitude that form the soil in which a spiritual life can be nurtured.

Two of my students videotaped a series of interviews with fellow students in which they were trying to determine the kinds of values motivating their peers. In one question addressed to the students being interviewed, they were asked what they would wish for if they had three wishes. In fourteen out of sixteen cases, the answer was "Lots of money." Of the remaining two, one asked for health, while the other, a very clever person, asked to have a thousand more wishes.

It's understandable that people aren't that interested in getting to know God. Those who speak for God turn people away by the thousands. Just yesterday I spoke with a young man who had recently attended a church service. His comment was: "After we were told for the eighth time what wretched sinners we were, I felt that I had enough church to last me for at least another year." I meet many "recovering Christians" trying to get over a legacy of guilt and shame. There are all too few voices in the religious marketplace helping us to understand what it means to "look at the living one while you live."

People who do evince some interest in God often fall prey to some hawker of religion who offers them a magic charm to get into heaven. "If you accept Jesus as your Lord and Savior" or "If you are baptized" or "If you say the prayer of Jabez" or "If you find the right crystal" or "If you chant the right mantra"—charms like these are peddled by myriad salespersons who all share a common characteristic. To them, our spiritual good is separate from who we are. Our salvation is in the mantra, or in Jesus or in the crystal, but it's never in ourselves.

If there is a golden thread weaving together these diverse teachings in the Gospel of Thomas, it is the realization that everything is in us now. Our spiritual reality does not reside somewhere else in space nor is it to be found anywhere else in time. It is here and now. As a Roman Catholic child, I learned the answers to the famous *Baltimore Catechism*. "Why did God make us?" "To know, love, and serve Him in this world and to be happy with Him in heaven." Notice the alienation implicit in this. Where does happiness lie? In heaven. Life is here but happiness is reserved for somewhere else and some other time, a place that is far away and a time after we die. It's never here and now.

Practice

Have you ever trained a puppy? Taken it out on a leash and tried to teach it to heel? That's nothing compared to training the mind. The Buddhists tell us the mind is like a chattering monkey on our shoulder. Or you might think of it as a video playing in our head. We wake up in the morning and it's already running and it's still running when we're ready to go to bed at night. The interesting thing about this video is that it's never showing where we are at the moment. It's always showing some other time and place. It's either back somewhere in the past or forward somewhere in the future.

When I taught high school for three years at a Jesuit boys' school, I often thought of those carnival games where you're trying to throw the ball at a moving target. There was so much hormonal energy in those young students that a teacher had to have good aim to strike home once in a while. When you did connect, it was exciting. For one fantastic moment, they were really there. They were in the here and now. Otherwise, they were sorting out the phone conversation they had had with their girlfriend the night before or anticipating the upcoming prom or football game that weekend.

Have you ever been with people who are never where they are? When you're having dinner with them, they're talking about the movie you're going to later that evening. During the movie, they're whispering to you about what they liked or didn't like at the dinner. On the way home from the movie, they're talking about work the next day. It's as though they were never where they were. Our undisciplined minds are a lot like that. They want to be everywhere except where we are. Like untrained puppies, they want to be everywhere but at our heels.

The first step in training the wayward mind is to realize that it is indeed wayward. The first step to living in the here and now is noticing that we don't. Try practicing that for a day or two. Don't do anything different. Just catch yourself now and again and ask yourself where your mind is. If you have one of those alarm clock watches, you can even set it for every hour or so and see the results. After a while, you'll start to notice without any external reminder. I was having lunch with a friend of mine who is a spiritual teacher. He spilled the salt. Tracing the small trail of salt granules with his finger he said, "My guru would have asked me where my mind was from here to here." See how many times you can find where your mind is in the course of a day or two of observation.

Reflections

1. How much of my day is spent mulling over the past or anticipating something in the future? How much time is left for the present?
2. When I notice that I'm not in the here and now, do I also notice that, even if it's only for a millisecond, that I am in the here and now?
3. Do I also notice that being in the now blends into itself? How now and here becomes now/here?

11

Marinating in Mystery

THIS CHAPTER IS NOT BASED ON ANY ONE PARTICULAR SAYING IN THE Gospel of Thomas but on an underlying premise of every saying—the reality and mystery of God. How can we move to an understanding of the Divine that is consonant with the profoundly spiritual tone of the Gospel of Thomas? My own way was paved by two great teachers, neither of whom I met personally, but each of whom continues to inform my faith and practice. These thinkers are Gabriel Marcel (1889–1973) and Rudolf Otto (1869–1937).[14]

I was pursuing graduate studies in philosophy at St. Louis University when a fellow student walked into my room one day to announce that Gabriel Marcel was giving a talk on campus. As it turned out, I missed his talk that day, but I was led to read one of his books. It was there that I encountered a distinction that helped me to articulate something I had intuited for a long time. It was from Gabriel Marcel that I first learned the crucial distinction between problem and mystery. A problem is something that, in principle, can be solved because it exists apart from us, objectified in some way or defined.

Now we all know about problem solving. It's what most education is about from the first time we are told to "solve for *x*." What Marcel reminds us of is that there are also mysteries. These are not Agatha Christie-type mysteries, for in the last analysis those are really problems. Who killed Colonel Mustard in the library with the knife? A mystery, in Marcel's sense, is not reducible to being a problem. It is not something that I can objectify, since it is something containing me. It cannot be placed outside of me, since I am inside it. A mystery, therefore, cannot be solved.

What, then, is the proper response to a mystery? Participation. It's the same word in Marcel's original French and in English. One doesn't solve a mystery; one participates in it. The mystery is not totally unknowable, but access to it cannot be obtained through the methodologies that prove so effective in problem solving. This participation is not a single act but a process, often a lifetime of loving "marination." Think of the way two friends or life partners might grow through the years, participating ever more deeply in each other's ontological mystery, that presence of the other's being that lies beyond all mere reasoning.

I remember being a colecturer in a graduate class with a colleague of mine from the psychology department. He announced at one point that he was an atheist. I asked him what might lead him to change that position. He informed me that I would have to give him scientific proof of God's existence. At this point, I recognized his personal unawareness of Marcel's distinction. I told him that I could not "solve" the problem by that kind of methodology but that if he were serious in wanting to know the divine reality, he might consider spending two or three months in a monastery (whether Buddhist, Hindu, or Christian), learning some of the disciplined ways of "participating" in the ultimate mystery. I don't think he was interested in taking me up on that challenge.

My second great teacher in these matters was Rudolf Otto, a renowned professor of religion for many years at the University of Marburg. I thought of him when I visited that lovely university town on a trip to Germany a few years ago with my son and daughter. Otto was not one to remain in his study all his life. He traveled extensively and interviewed shamans and witch doctors, priests and prophets, mystics and seers all over the world. He also studied the literature in the world's sacred traditions.

The result of all of this research was his classic work *Das Heilige,* "The Holy." What Otto discovered underlying all the world's religions was what Marcel called a mystery, a primary experience, something not reducible to any other category. It was an experience he described as numinous, coming from the Latin word, *numen,* an ancient word for the Divine, especially as it is present in nature.

Behind those words *numinous* and *numen* is a root meaning "to nod." It is as though there were a divine reality in everything and everyone, and occasionally it nods to us. And if we are alert, we will turn aside to notice it. It is much like Moses in chapter 3 of Exodus, "turning aside" to see the bush that is burning and yet not consumed. The rabbis tell us that if Moses had not "turned aside," the redemption of Israel might not have been accomplished. And so it is whenever we sense the numinous: We are called to turn aside. It is only then that we can participate in the mystery of the holy.

Moses was told to take off his shoes in the presence of the numinous, and this sentiment is shared by people all over the world when they sense themselves to be in the presence of the holy. This mystery of the holy, present wherever there is religion, involves an ambivalent response on the part of human beings, and that led Otto to use the Latin phrase *mysterium tremendum et fascinans*—a mystery at once overwhelming and attractive. In other words, we are both drawn to this mystery of the holy and, at the same time, afraid of it. We are like Peter, as he is described in the fifth chapter of Luke's gospel. After seeing Jesus's power over the forces of nature, Peter asks Jesus to depart from him because he is a sinner. And yet, there is no one to whom Peter is more drawn. This very ambivalence lies at the heart of the encounter with the holy.

So this "God" of our investigation is not someone to be known through a rational methodology but someone to be experienced through participation. But before we pursue further the ways of participating in the divine mystery, we need to perform one more purification in our ordinary God talk. Many people tend to speak of God mostly as He; some today prefer She. But God is neither He nor

She nor It. God is not an entity at all. In other words, if you are sitting with two friends in a room and God enters the room, this three and one does not equal four.

I first learned to grapple with this insight when I was studying Thomas Aquinas, a great thirteenth-century philosopher, writing at a time when Jewish, Muslim, and Christian thinkers participated in a high level of theological dialogue. Aquinas taught that God was not a being among beings. God was the "to be" in every being, the heart of reality, the eternal spring from which all reality pours out. This finds classic expression for me in the first verse of an untitled and unfinished poem by the English Jesuit poet Gerard Manley Hopkins (1844–1889):

Thee, God, I come from, to thee go,
All dáy long I like fountain flow
From thy hand out, swayed about
Mote-like in thy mighty glow.[15]

God is not another thing in the universe, not a noun. God is more like the infinitive form of the verb "to be." In other words, that form of a verb that is least bound by person, number, and gender: to see, to walk, to know. *Infinitive* means "no limit" and thus serves as a good metaphor for the Infinite One. From the day I learned that God was not a being among beings but *Esse Subsistens,* subsistent to-be-ness, I have never been attracted to atheism. For most atheism consists in the denial of another being somewhere in the universe, in heaven perhaps where an old man sits on a throne of clouds. No, God is rather the to-be-ness of everything that is.

Does this mean that God is simply an impersonal force or energy? Not at all. The Hindus say that the ultimate reality is *Satchitananda.* That means truth, consciousness, and bliss. God is not a personality; God is trans-personal. But God is present to us in a way that is personal. God resides in all that is true, all that is aware, all that knows the joy of existence. Most important, God is here and now. God is in fact the Eternal Now.

Practice

We come now to the question of practice. How do we begin to marinate in the mystery of the Divine? We must create for ourselves a place and time of silence and solitude, a sacred space and a sacred time. As we make spiritual progress, eventually all space and all times will be sacred; but there are stages of growth in the life of the Spirit as in all other things.

The Buddhists tell us that at first mountains are mountains and trees are trees. Then there comes a point when mountains are no longer mountains and trees no longer trees. Finally, mountains are mountains and trees trees. What is the key to this conundrum? Our first consciousness is unconsciousness. We live in the world without awareness or attention, taking things for granted. It's just another day, another sunrise, another meal, another job. This is the house of unconsciousness most of us inhabit most of the time. Mountains are mountains and trees are trees ... what's new!

But then something "nods" at us. We sense the numinous, the mystery of the holy. Perhaps it happens when we're looking at the sky or listening to music or talking to a friend. It can happen anywhere, at any time. But it's a moment when we turn aside; we notice; we wonder; we are amazed. This, in turn, leads us to begin a practice, trying to be more aware, more attentive, more of the time. Now we enter a time of disturbance, perhaps even a period of cognitive dissonance. Things look strange to us. What is really happening in this moment at hand? Why is this tree here? Why am I here? Why is there something rather than nothing? Now mountains are no longer mountains and trees no longer trees. We stop taking things for granted and start to notice.

The Sufis, Muslim mystics, employ a similar tripartite model. The three stages on the Sufi path are sobriety, drunkenness, and sobriety. As in the Buddhist schema, the first and third, though semantically identical, are not the same. The initial sobriety is a level where we begin to pay attention and reform our morals. The stage of drunkenness corresponds to a trans-rational state where the divine reality radically transforms experience. And the third stage of sobriety after drunkenness is the return to the healthy ordinariness of existence, a return to the world where one is in the world but not of it.

As we advance on the spiritual path, enlightenment embraces all that is. There is an experienced integrity in all we experience, all that we will, all that we do. Mountains are indeed mountains. Trees are indeed trees. But, oh, what a difference in meaning from those same words when we uttered them at that unconscious, half-asleep stage of our lives. Now all is bright. Now all is miraculous. For we have learned that miracles are not unusual events but events to which we have learned to pay unusual attention.

Now all of this can happen anytime and anywhere. But for most of us it helps in the early stages of our journey to drive a wedge into our workaday world by creating some sacred time and sacred space. Let's start with the space. We have a meditation room at the college where I teach. It's a wonderful room, filled with the smell of incense and scented candles, carpeted in silence and peace. If you are blessed with a large home, you might want to set aside a whole room to create such a space for yourself, remembering, of course, always to take your shoes off before entering it.

But if your living environment is smaller, create a nook or corner, a shelf or little space. I have such a shelf in my office and in my home. It may help to have one special chair that you use for practice. Perhaps it has a particularly nice view of the world outside or is otherwise attractive to you. And the room or shelf or table might have a candle on it or pictures of people or places that inspire you to spiritual growth or texts that draw you to a deeper place in yourself—a Bible or a Qur'an, for example, or a statue of the Buddha or of Mary.

Now that you have a space, make a time. You'll notice that I said "making time" and not "having time." A good discipline for beginning practice is to catch ourselves talking about what we don't "have" time to do. I find that I increase my self-honesty if I talk instead about what I'm not "making" time to do. We will never "have" time for any of the practices talked about in this book, but we can "make" time for them if they become priorities in our life.

What, then, are we making time for? We want to marinate in the divine mystery without being sidetracked by the images with which we have been socialized to talk about God. We recognize the metaphoric power of calling God "Father" or "Mother" or "Shepherd" or "our Rock," but we know that these are metaphors, not literal descriptions. They highlight certain aspects of the way we experience the divine mystery: as loving parent (Father/Mother), as guiding mentor (Shepherd), as reliable foundation (Rock). But we want to transcend those metaphors now and enter into the deeper experience of the divine reality.

There are various forms of spiritual practice that we will discuss in these pages.[16] At this point, I want to discuss only one of these myriad practices: the practice of noncognitive meditation. Ours is such a hectic, even frenetic, society. Our minds are like muddied waters where distractions are stirred up in every moment. Noncognitive meditation means not thinking, not conceptualizing, not reasoning, not worrying. We just need a place to sit (remember that sacred space you created) and make some time, a quarter of an hour for openers.

Sit in that special chair (or in a yoga position if you are comfortable with that). Keep your back straight and your feet on the floor. Bring your hands together. Close your eyes. Take a few cleansing breaths and just sit still. It's good to sit still. It's good to just breathe. A friend of mine has a sign over her desk: Don't just do something, stand there. In our culture, this is subversive but necessary wisdom. By just sitting there in silence, we are doing something dramatically countercultural. The TV is off; the cell phone is off; the computer is off; but our consciousness is on.

If you try this for a few minutes, you will find yourself going crazy with thoughts and impulses. So we're going to add one more ingredient to this mixture: a sacred phrase. Since this chapter is about God, let's begin with this phrase: Be still and know that I am God. You might say that line out loud a few times and then internalize it and let it be sounded quietly in your heart. After a few minutes, shorten the phrase and say: Be still and know that I am. After a few more minutes, shorten the phrase even more and say: Be still and know. And after yet another few minutes, simply say: Be still. Repeat these phrases until the timer on your watch tells you that the fifteen minutes are over. Breathe deeply, gently open your eyes, and go on with your day.

What are the best times to do this? Mornings, if possible. The first step on the spiritual path may be setting your alarm fifteen minutes earlier. Morning practice is good because it sets our whole day on a good course. But other times work as well. Fit the practice to the exigencies of your day. If you can make time for another quarter of an hour in your day, take advantage of it. Remember, the best is the enemy of the good. Our goal is not perfection, but improvement. Five minutes is better than nothing. But do it with some regularity and you will notice a difference.

Repetition is the technical word sometimes used for taking the sacred phrase into the rest of your day. There are so many little vacant spots in our day: standing in supermarket lines, folding laundry, doing dishes, sitting in traffic. Instead of stirring up our stomach acids, we can learn to see these times as opportunities for quiet practice, ways of quietly learning "to see the living one while we are alive."

With this simple practice we will inevitably find, step by step and day by day, that our hearts are softened and opened, the turbulence of our life subsides, and we experience greater peace. We no longer look for proof of some divine entity sitting on a distant star. The Divine, the mystery of the holy, is within and around us more and more. We no longer simply believe in God, we know God with an interior knowing that is both experiential and transformative.

Reflections

1. Can I create a sacred space in my living and/or work environment? What do I want to put there?
2. Can I make time in my busy life for a few minutes of noncognitive meditation? What will it entail?
3. Can I take a "sacred phrase" into the rest of my day? Where do I find spaces to use it—while sitting in traffic, folding laundry, standing in a checkout line?

12

Jesus for Christians and Non-Christians

ONCE I HAD A DREAM IN WHICH I SAW ONE OF THOSE TRADITIONAL statues of Jesus that Catholics call the "Sacred Heart." His hands were outstretched, his heart visible on his tunic. Around his neck was a sign that said, "Church Property." In my dream, I knew I must get to that sign and take it off. I woke up before I was able to manage that. Maybe this chapter will help my dream come true.

13 Jesus asked his disciples: Make a comparison; what am I like? Simon Peter replied: You are like a righteous messenger. Matthew replied: You are like an intelligent lover of wisdom. Thomas replied: Teacher, I cannot possibly say what you are like. Jesus said to Thomas: I am not your teacher; you have drunk from and become intoxicated from the bubbling water that I poured out. Jesus took Thomas and they withdrew. Jesus said three things to him. When Thomas returned to the other disciples, they asked him: What did Jesus tell you? Thomas replied: If I tell you even one of the things that he told me, you would pick up stones and throw them at me, and fire would come out of those stones and burn you up.

The question of Jesus's identity is one of the central themes of this chapter. It was a central issue for his disciples during the brief time of his teaching ministry. In Mark's gospel, as in the later gospels of Matthew and Luke that use Mark as a source, a scene comparable to the one described in saying 13 forms the very center of the narrative (Mark 8:27–30). There the disciples are wondering if he might be Elijah returned (for in the biblical account Elijah did not die but was taken to heaven in a fiery chariot) or one of the other prophets come back to earth. Peter finally trumps the other disciples by declaring Jesus to be the Christ, the Anointed One of God, the Messiah.

In saying 13, although the scene is commensurate, we have an entirely different kind of dialogue. Here there is no identification of Jesus with one of the prominent figures in the Hebrew Bible, not even with the promised Messiah. Simon Peter calls him one "like a righteous messenger." To be righteous is to be God-centered; this translates the Hebrew *zedek* and the Greek *dikaios*, both of which mean to be in a right relationship with God and with one's fellow human beings. In the Qur'an, twenty-five prophets are listed, five of whom are considered messengers: Noah, Abraham, Moses, Jesus, and Muhammad. Messengers have a special calling to deliver God's Word to their contemporaries, even more so than the other prophets.

Matthew calls Jesus "an intelligent lover of wisdom." This is an appropriate answer to attribute to Matthew, since the gospel that carries his name has more of Jesus's teachings than any other single source. In Matthew, Jesus is clearly a teacher of wisdom. Matthew contains five separate collections of wisdom teachings, corresponding to the Five Books of Moses (the Torah or Pentateuch) in the Hebrew Bible. Matthew's answer is true but not adequate to the way of knowing that the Gospel of Thomas encourages us to experience.

The third answer, which is no answer at all, comes from Thomas. This is, by the way, the only place that Thomas appears in the Gospel of Thomas. Although pleading a total inability to describe what Jesus is like, Thomas nonetheless addresses him as "Teacher." Jesus objects to this title, telling Thomas that he has himself drunk of the bubbling waters that Jesus poured out. This is a very important theme in the Gospel of Thomas. It is basic to the idea of being Jesus's twin. Jesus does not want to set up a superior/inferior relationship. Not denying that he does indeed pour out the bubbling water, he wants the focus to remain on what Thomas has done—namely, drunk from and become intoxicated by that water.

This is one of the key differences between the Gospel of Thomas and the kind of hierarchical religion that thrives in the soil of our collective egos. The split between clergy and laity is a constant in many forms of religion. Thomas Believers reject all second-class status in community membership, whether among believers or between the believer and any external authority (Jesus or the Buddha, pope or patriarch). There is a radical egalitarianism here that does not sit well with those who see religion as a means of manipulating others, controlling them through shame and guilt, and putting most people down to exalt the role of some privileged leader or clerical caste.

The most mysterious part of this exchange in saying 13 is when Jesus takes Thomas aside and tells him three things. When Thomas is asked about what Jesus has told him, he replies that if he revealed even one of them, the disciples would want to stone him and fire would come out of the stones to burn them up. These punishments imply that the content of those three sayings would be considered blasphemous. What might that blasphemy be? I think it is clearly the very ideas that lead many contemporary Christians to reject this gospel as heretical—namely, the realization that Jesus is different from us, not in kind, but in degree.

Fundamentalists are often wont to ask people, "Do you believe that Jesus is God?" I always respond happily in the affirmative. What they fail to do, however, is to pose the follow-up question: "Do you believe that Jesus is God in a different way than you are God?" It is there that I would have to respond in the negative. Jesus in the Gospel of Thomas is not here to redeem or rescue people from their hopeless bondage to some kind of original sin. He is here rather to remind people that they are indeed God, as he himself is. This is true, of course, of the higher consciousness in Jesus and in ourselves, the Christ consciousness or the Buddha nature. To claim divinity for the ego would be insanity.

I spent some twenty years studying the sayings attributed to Jesus in the gospels and other early Christian writings. This resulted in three books: *Wisdom of the Carpenter, The Hidden Gospel of Matthew: Annotated and Explained* (SkyLight Paths), and the guidebook you are reading. Beyond these publications, however, this study gave me a sense of "the authentic voice of Jesus." I can, of course, be wrong. My sense of Jesus remains partial, provisional, and perspectival. But the clear result of this study was the removal for me of the two roadblocks to Christian pluralism I mentioned in the Introduction. I found no evidence that Jesus was "the only begotten Son of the Father" and I found nothing in his teachings corresponding to what is later called original sin.

Now this assertion will seem absurd to many Christians, and they will rush forward to quote a plethora of scriptural statements to the contrary, statements affirming that Jesus is indeed the only begotten Son of the Father and that his atoning death for our inherent sinful condition was the motivating factor for his whole mission. The key issue here, of course, lies in how we read the Bible. If we see the gospels, for example, as layered works in which earlier traditions of sayings were complemented by later sayings stemming from the Christian community, then it is quite possible to conclude that a particular saying has a later setting than the historical life-world of Jesus himself. If, however, we read the gospels as eyewitness accounts of Jesus's life and teaching, then these contrary claims seem to represent the grossest kind of error.

I am impressed by the gospel tradition that when Jesus was praised by someone, even in such a simple matter as being called "good teacher," he reprimanded his interlocutor, reminding him that "no one is good but God" (Mark 10:18). In those sayings with the highest probability of having been spoken by Jesus, he seems to deflect attention from himself and point to God. And when he does point to the divine reality within himself, I see it not as a way of differentiating himself from others, but as a way of inviting others to recognize their own deeper reality.

Peccatum originale (original sin) is a term first found in the writings of the fourth-century theologian Augustine of Hippo. It seems to be based on some of Paul's interpretations of the Adam and Eve story. The famous "Fall of Adam" in Christian vocabulary is unknown to both Jews and Muslims, although their sacred scriptures contain the story of Adam and Eve's disobedience. The Hebrew scriptures do assert that sin lies at the door for all of us and that it is our inclination, just as the Qur'an declares that human beings were created weak. But neither this inclination (of which Jews speak) nor this weakness (of which Muslims speak) alienates human beings from God or renders a relationship with God impossible without some kind of atoning sacrifice.

In meditating upon Jesus's death on the cross at the hands of the Roman imperial system (the ancient creed states that Jesus suffered "under Pontius Pilate," the Roman procurator at the time), Christians saw that death in the light of certain passages from the Hebrew Bible, especially references in Isaiah to God's "suffering servant," one faithful to God who is persecuted and yet helps others by his suffering. Consider, for example, Isaiah 53:5: "But he was pierced for our transgression, crushed for our iniquities; the chastisement he bore restored us to health and by his wounds we are healed."

In the traditional religions of Asia, we also find the idea that highly enlightened beings elevate the human community by their suffering. Having completed their own karmic journey, they return to the world to take on the karmic burden of the larger community of humankind. As long as one uses these metaphors lightly, they provide legitimate insight into the martyrdom of figures like Jesus, Gandhi, and Martin Luther King Jr. But when this kind of image becomes the controlling metaphor for understanding a martyr's death, then an imbalance sets in, a distortion. Much of contemporary Christianity, especially in its fundamentalist forms, suffers from this imbalance.

The metaphor of a sacrificial death does not appear at all in the Gospel of Thomas. It is not part of the Thomas Believer's story of faith.

The elevation of this useful metaphor to center stage in Christian theology has led to distortions on a grand scale. I remember to this day how I first heard the story from Sister Imelda in the fourth grade. Adam and Eve committed a terrible sin and God shut the door of heaven in anger. How could the door be opened again? Someone would have to make atonement. And since the sin was against God, the atoning sacrifice had to be made by someone who was himself divine. But since the sin was committed by human beings, the sacrifice had to be made by someone who was human. So God the Father looked around and realized that only his Son fit the description. He, therefore, sent his Son to earth to die this terrible death on the cross. When Jesus had poured out his last drop of blood, God's wrath was appeased and he once again opened the gates of heaven.

Having a penchant for theology, even in the fourth grade, I raised my hand at that point and said to Sister Imelda: "I don't think my father would have done it that way." Needless to say, Sister Imelda was not happy with my answer and she immediately taped my mouth shut with masking tape. This happened to me frequently and was particularly distressing because the combination of a deviated septum and allergies often made it difficult for me to breathe through my nose. A compassionate classmate took pity on me and made a hole through the tape with the point of her compass and I was able to suck in air for the remainder of the class. I thus escaped my first heresy trial.

With apologies to Sister Imelda and all who have taught this doctrine from the time of Anselm, I must continue to disagree.[17] My father would not have done it that way, nor would my God. The whole story had become a travesty and, as James Carroll points out in his brilliant work *Constantine's Sword,* the cross replaced Easter as Christianity's center.[18] And the good news of the transformation of death into life now became decisively bad news, a brutal weapon in the fight to convert everyone to the truth of this story.

It had never been Jesus's story, but that no longer made a difference. It had become the master story through which Christian empires could be built. And, more important, it was a story through which Christian exclusivism could be propagated and Christian guilt perpetuated. For no one could get to heaven without benefit of this atoning death and no one could access the power of this death without submitting to the authority of the Church.

> **61b Salome asked him: Who are you, man? As though coming from someone, you have come onto my couch and eaten from my table. Jesus replied: I am he who comes into being from him who is the same. Some of the things of my Father have been given to me. [Salome said:] I am your disciple.**

We know little about Salome, except for her identification in Mark as one of the women "looking on from a distance" (Mark 15:40) as Jesus died on the cross. We are told that these women "used to follow him and provided for him when he was in Galilee" (Mark 15:41). The final reference to her occurs in the sixteenth chapter of Mark, where we are told that she was one of the women who went to the tomb on Sunday morning to anoint the body of Jesus, one of the women who saw the young man dressed in white who told them that Jesus was raised from the dead and that they should tell the disciples that Jesus had gone ahead of them to the Galilee, one of the women who fled from the tomb in terror and amazement. Matthew, although he uses over 90 percent of Mark in writing his gospel, omits Salome's name from the list of women who stood at the cross, as well as the women who went to the tomb. So does Luke.

In saying 61b, she is clearly one of Jesus's disciples, someone in the Galilee who had offered Jesus hospitality. He sat on her couch and ate from her table. What I find interesting is Jesus's claim that: "*Some* of the things of my Father have been given to me" (emphasis is mine). The implication seems to be that other things have not been given to him. This is clearly not a picture of Jesus as the exclusive channel of divine wisdom. Perhaps some of God's truth resides only in the Buddha, or only in Muhammad, or only in you or me. There's a humility in the faith of Thomas Believers that is prominently absent in the more exclusivist religions.

> **62a Jesus said: I tell my mysteries to people worthy of my mysteries.**

There's an old Latin adage in scholastic philosophy: *Quidquid recipitur, recipitur per modum recipientis.* Loosely translated: "Whatever is received, is received according to the capacity of the recipient." Saying 62a can be understood in the context of saying 93 in which Jesus tells his hearers not to give "holy things to dogs" or "pearls to pigs." We find a similar image in one of the sayings attributed to Muhammad: "Seeking knowledge is incumbent on every Muslim: he who offers knowledge to those who do not appreciate it is like the one who decorates pigs with precious stones, pearls and gold."[19] These sayings stress the fact that we human beings have to take some responsibility for making ourselves receptive soil for the seed God wants to plant in us. If we don't make that fundamental effort, then those trying to help us are wasting their time.

> **77a Jesus said: I am the light above everything. I am everything. Everything came forth from me, and everything reached me.**

> **77b Split wood, I am there. Lift up a rock, you will find me there.**

This is one of the most celebrated sayings in the Gospel of Thomas. It sounds pantheistic to most readers, but it contains the deepest message of mystical religion. Only God is real. From the higher consciousness that Jesus embodies and that he invites us to attain, there is only God. Transcending the ego with its ever-changing agenda, Thomas Believers, like Jesus, come to identify with that deep place in themselves that is the reality of God. They know themselves then at the beginning of the whole process of the One manifesting itself as many and at the end of the process when the many are folded back into the One. Where can God be found? How can we know the essential nature of Jesus? Where can we find our deepest selves? Split wood. Lift up a rock. Dig down into the soil on which you stand. Everything is there.

> **91 They said to him: Tell us who you are so that we can believe in you. He replied: You analyze the appearance of the sky and the earth, but you don't recognize what is right in front of you, and you don't know the nature of the present time.**

Saying 91 brings us again to the necessity of attention and awareness. Everything is there in the here and now but we ourselves are absent. St. Augustine made this same point in his *Confessions,* saying to God: *Tu eras intus; ego autem foras.* In a free English translation: "You, God, were inside of me, but I was outside of myself." In other words, our normal condition is so distracted that we can't recognize what is right in front of us, what is happening in the present moment. We are absent to our own interior life; and, therefore, it is as if that life does not exist.

What does Jesus mean by "the nature of the present time"? Greek has two words for time: *chronos* and *kairos.* The former is clock time, like half past seven. The latter is opportune time, like the time when the fruit becomes ripe or when the pregnant woman is delivered of her child. Theologians speak of *kairotic time,* and it is that kind of time that is being alluded to here. How can we learn to live more in kairotic time? One way is through the cultivation of silence and solitude that we spoke of in the last chapter, that sacred time and space where we can practice noncognitive meditation.

> **100 They showed Jesus a gold coin and said: Caesar's agents demand that we pay his taxes. He replied: Give to Caesar what is Caesar's. Give to God what is God's. And give me what is mine.**

This saying, narrated in the canonical gospels as well, is central to Jesus's mission and message. Jesus has no concern about paying taxes.

Since the gold coins bear Caesar's image, one might as well give them back to Caesar. But as we know from Genesis 1:26, human beings are made in God's image and likeness. Therefore, what bears God's image should be returned to God. This is what Jesus's mission was about—facilitating that return of human beings to God. The final phrase of saying 100, "And give me what is mine," is not found in the canonical gospels and seems to destroy the classic parallelism of the balanced teaching regarding Caesar and God. I would judge it, therefore, to be a later addition.

105 Jesus said: One who knows the father and the mother will be called the son of a whore.

This may be the most important saying in the Gospel of Thomas when it comes to giving us information about Jesus's background. The women of dubious character included by Matthew in his genealogy of Jesus, as well as the midrashic (i.e., sermonic commentary) story of Jesus's birth by a virgin (a story found in Matthew and Luke but not in Mark, John, or Paul) seem to rest on some irregularity about Jesus's birth. A later Jewish polemic claims that Mary had been raped by a Roman soldier and that Jesus was therefore born illegitimately.

Perhaps Jesus was called "the son of a whore." Stephen Mitchell sees Jesus's experience of being marginalized as a bastard in his home community as the root of his later compassion for others similarly marginalized: women, the poor, the diseased.[20] Being made fun of as a bastard helped to soften Jesus's own heart toward others who were mocked, despised, and rejected. Jane Schaberg explores Jesus's illegitimacy, finding there a new source of Mary's true greatness as well as her son's compassion.[21]

According to saying 105, Jesus knows his mother and father. This may have a twofold meaning. He knows that Mary and Joseph are his parents. But he also knows his deeper parentage, the true origin of each one of us: the heavenly Father and Mother Wisdom. Jesus's birth was indeed as natural as any other human birth. The midrash in Luke and Matthew points through a poetic image to his deeper origin in

God. And that origin is ours as well. In this symbolic sense, we all derive from a virgin birth.

> **108 Jesus said: He who drinks from my mouth will become like I am, and I will become he. And the hidden things will be revealed to him.**

The final saying we are considering in this chapter highlights the theme of Jesus's twin. We will become like Jesus. He will become us. The smaller ego is displaced by the Christ self that lives in us, just as Jesus's ego was similarly engulfed in the reality of the Christ consciousness. Every spiritual path involves the diminution of the ego and the rising of "the Christ" in us. This, of course, has other names in other traditions; Buddhists, for example, speak of it as "the Buddha nature." The point is that unless we transcend the small self (the ego) and enter into the larger reality of our divine identity, the hidden things cannot be revealed to us. If one says, "I am God" from the ego self, that is delusion; but if one says it from the larger self, it is profoundly true. And this happens to Jesus's twins because they drink from Jesus's mouth. They go to the source of living water, the awareness of their divine identity.

Practice

How can we put into practice this new understanding of Jesus? First of all, we need to let go of the worship of Jesus. He was not among us to be worshiped but to be imitated. He did not want us to depend on him but to learn from him. His purpose was not to do something instead of us but to help us to understand what we can and indeed must do for ourselves. He did not want our praise but our practice. The Buddhists state this most strongly: "If you meet the Buddha on the path, kill him." In other words, if you see your spiritual reality as somehow alienated from you—in another person (even the Buddha or the Christ) or in an infallible text or a cult leader or a crystal—then you must destroy it.

There is an adage in my field of comparative religions that every religion is best by virtue of something that it does. Certainly Christianity is best in celebrating Jesus as a model of compassionate outreach to the most marginalized members of society. This brings me, then, to speak of the practice I would suggest relating to this second part of our creed. How can we become messengers of God's Word, bringers of God's healing, and hearts of God's compassion?

We spoke earlier of the seven chakras, and Jesus has quite naturally been identified primarily with the heart chakra. Understanding Jesus in terms of the heart chakra gives new meaning to much of my education as a Roman Catholic. I was taught by the Missionary Sisters of the Sacred Heart. The statue of the Sacred Heart was prominent in the school where I received my education—I mentioned it also in the dream with which I began this chapter. In these statues, the heart of Jesus is visible on his chest. This makes a great deal of symbolic sense, since there is no real spirituality without the activation of the heart chakra. Religion at its best is always a path of the heart. People in whom the heart chakra has not begun to turn are incapable of altruism or compassion.

One of the first prayers I learned from the sisters who taught me was "Jesus meek and humble of heart, make my heart like unto Thine." This phrase can be used as the sacred phrase during meditation or as the form of repetition in those other times of the day that make no demands on us for cognitive activity. Meekness and humility are often misunderstood but they are in fact virtues most desperately needed at every level of our society today. A meek and gentle heart indicates an activated heart chakra.

Meekness means gentleness of spirit and the ability of the heart to soften. It is the opposite of the *hard-heartedness* so prevalent in our dog-eat-dog world. And *humility* in its root meaning (the Latin word *humus*, meaning "ground" or "earth") grounds us, helps us to keep our feet on the floor, keeps us from false pride and arrogance. When traveling in Europe over the summer of 2003, I heard the word *arrogant* used most often to describe the way our political and military leadership appears to the world. The Chinese tell us that the ocean is the greatest body of water because it lies the lowest, thus enabling it to receive all the rivers of the world. To be meek and humble is an important challenge for Americans today.

If you find yourself comfortable with this Heart Prayer, you may use it in your noncognitive practice. Say the prayer out loud two or three times and then internalize it, letting it be the focus of your attention for fifteen or twenty minutes. You may then take it into your day, using it in all those noncognitive spaces you will readily find in the course of a day. "Jesus meek and humble of heart, make my heart like unto Thine" provides a gentle means for activating the heart chakra.

If this particular prayer does not appeal to you, you might consider some of the phrases that occur in the gospels or in other sacred prayers or writings, including some of the phrases in the Gospel of Thomas. "I cannot say what you are like." "Let me drink from your mouth." "I am your disciple." "Teach me to love." "Lord, that I may see." "Lord, make me an instrument of your peace." Any one of these can be used as a sacred phrase, plus countless others that you can find on your own. The main idea is to find a phrase encapsulating for you the special quality that makes Jesus important for you.

Reflections

1. Even if I do not describe myself as a Christian, do I see Jesus as a model in my spiritual quest?
2. What qualities of Jesus's life and teachings do I want to incorporate into my own spiritual path?
3. What are some concrete steps I can take to become more "meek and humble of heart"?

13

Making Space for the Spirit

10 Jesus said: I have thrown fire on the world. Look! I watch it until it blazes.

IT'S NOT CERTAIN THAT THIS FIRE REFERS TO THE HOLY SPIRIT BUT I THINK there are legitimate grounds for interpreting it that way. It's important to remember that the word *spirit* also means *wind* or *breath* in Hebrew, Greek, and Latin. These languages are gendered languages and it's interesting that the word for *spirit* is feminine in Hebrew, neuter in Greek, and masculine in Latin. This affects the tonality of the concept and even its visualization. In an early mosaic representation of the Trinity, for example, the Holy Spirit is clearly a woman with breasts. This tells us that the artist knew Hebrew.

From the beginning of the biblical story, God's Spirit is the dynamic presence of God in the world. In Genesis 1:2, the *ruach elohim,* the spirit (or wind or breath) of God, moves over the face of the primordial waters of creation, bringing cosmos out of the preceding chaos. This creation is clearly not a *creatio ex nihilo* (creation from nothing) since God does not create either the preexisting water or the darkness. The initial divine action is rather one of separation and organization; and it is God's Spirit that directs this creative activity.

In First Samuel 10:10 we are told that Saul was met by a band of prophets "and the spirit of God possessed him, and he fell into a prophetic frenzy along with them." Here again we see the dynamic and powerful effects of God's Spirit. After Jesus's death and his appearance to his disciples as alive and risen, the Acts of the Apostles 2:2–3 describes the early community of believers gathered together, when "suddenly from heaven there came a sound like the rush of a violent wind, and it filled the entire house where they were sitting. Divided tongues, as of fire, appeared among them, and a tongue rested on each of them." Here we find the "wind" from Genesis, the element of violence as in Saul's frenzy, and the image of fire, the same image Jesus uses in saying 10.

In saying 82, Jesus says: "Whoever is near me is near the fire. Whoever is far from me is far from the Kingdom." This would suggest that the fire can also be identified with God's reign. The only difference between these two sayings lies in the fact that in saying 10 Jesus is throwing fire on the world and watching it until it blazes, whereas in saying 82 Jesus simply identifies himself with the fire. It is this distinctive dynamism in saying 10 that leads me to identify this fire with God's Spirit. There is even a kind of prototrinitarianism implicit here. God's reign (the Father/Mother) is embodied in Jesus (the Son/Daughter) and is being thrown (God's Spirit) on the world. As we noted earlier, the "persons" of the Trinity are not distinct personalities but ways in which the divine activity is experienced—in this case, as God's reign, Christ's presence, and the Spirit's action.

> **44 Jesus said: Whoever blasphemes against the Father will be forgiven. Whoever blasphemes against the son will be forgiven. But whoever blasphemes against the Holy Spirit will not be forgiven, neither on earth nor in heaven.**

This saying is found in the canonical gospels and has long presented a conundrum to scholars of the Christian Testament. What is the sin that cannot be forgiven? It seems to me that the clue to answering this question lies in the mention of the Holy Spirit. As we have seen, the Holy Spirit translates into God's action in the world. To blaspheme against the Holy Spirit is to take a stand against God's work in the world. This negates the possibility of forgiveness, since forgiveness is a primary work of God among us. The rabbis tell us that life would be unbearable had God not created forgiveness before he created the world. There is a saying of Muhammad that for the one who does "evil foolishly and repents afterwards thereof and does right, (for him) indeed, Allah is Forgiving, Merciful."[22] But however much forgiveness is God's nature and desire, pitting oneself against the very source of that forgiveness closes the doors of God's mercy both on earth and in heaven.

> **70 Jesus said: When you give rise to that which is within you, what you have will save you. If you do not give rise to it, what you do not have will destroy you.**

Davies rightly comments that what is within us is the light of the first day of creation.[23] In Genesis 1:3, God creates light as his first creation. And yet, it is not until the fourth day of creation that the sun and the moon are created. The rabbis long pondered the nature of this earlier light not emanating from the sun or the moon. They concluded that this is the mystical light, the light of creation before the first sin, before creation is darkened by the clouds of human ignorance and unwise choices. This becomes a metaphor, then, for a particular kind of consciousness, what I have called *Eden consciousness* in other writings. This, of course, is the kind of consciousness Jesus manifests, the consciousness from which he lives and teaches and acts in the world. When we allow that kind of consciousness to arise in us, it will save us. It is God's Spirit in us.

We notice here the lack of alienation in the Gospel of Thomas. We are not saved by something or someone outside of us. We are saved by something within us: Eden consciousness, Christ consciousness, the Buddha nature, the Mahatma (great soul), the Tao, the Holy Spirit. This is a transformative knowing, a *gnosis*. It is only through this that we are saved, that is, made whole, healthy, holy.

Many years ago, I heard the phrase "Holiness is wholeness," and that has resonated with me ever since. There is no shortcut to this, nothing else we can do instead of this. We either experience this transformation or we do not. No sacrament can give this to us; no priestly blessing can ensure its presence; no magic phrase or formula can force it to arise. The Spirit is always here and now.

Practice

How can we bring this awareness of the Holy Spirit to our practice? First of all, we have to keep in mind that the Holy Spirit is not a distinct personality. It is God's work in the world and in us. Just as you might watch a woman working in her garden or a man preparing dinner in the kitchen, the work is inseparable from the person. As we learn to pay attention to God's work in the world, I will introduce a fourth practice: guided meditation.

One form of guided meditation entails having an external guide. I often use this kind of guided meditation in retreats, when I guide others through the meditation. But it is completely possible to guide yourself in such a meditation. But whether you or another is the guide, the key ingredient is the use of the imagination. Here I will share a few guided meditations that you can lead yourself through in a fifteen- or twenty-minute period. The preparation for this exercise is the same as for the noncognitive meditation, that is, correct posture, normal breathing, closed eyes.

In the first exercise, imagine yourself stepping into an elevator on the seventh floor. You press the button for the ground floor and watch the elevator slowly descend floor by floor. When you exit the elevator, you are in a beautiful space. Imagine it in all its details. Then find a comfortable place to sit. You notice coming toward you someone who will be your guide. This can be someone alive or dead, someone real or fictional, someone you know or an archetypal form, a human being or an angel.

You welcome the guide and invite the guide to sit with you. Then you ask this guide a question. What am I meant to learn today? What is the meaning of what I'm experiencing in my life right now? Which way should I go in this decision that is facing me?

It is essential to this meditation to listen for an answer, recognizing that the answer may not be in words. The answer may be in a gesture or an expression of your guide or it may consist of an object the guide gives you. Simply be attentive to what happens after you ask your question. When you have received a response, spend some time pondering it. Then say good-bye to your guide and slowly return to the elevator, pressing the button for the seventh floor and feeling yourself gradually ascend. When you have ended the meditation, you might want to write down a few thoughts or reflections about the experience. It's not a bad idea to keep a journal to record your responses to these various practices.

In the second exercise, you begin the same way: the elevator, the walk through the beautiful scene, the comfortable seat. Only this time you are not meeting a guide, but yourself. Imagine yourself five years younger and meet that younger self, talking to that younger you and telling yourself what you need to know about the future that your younger self has not yet experienced. Continue meeting, greeting, talking to, and saying good-bye to your many selves, going back each time five years earlier, trying to identify yourself at that age through a memory of your birthday that year or something else special that happened. Your last visitor is yourself just moments after your birth. A nurse hands you to yourself and you look down at the newborn you, talking to this tiny being about all that lies ahead. After this last encounter, return the same way as in the earlier exercise.

One of the classic meditation texts is *The Spiritual Exercises of St. Ignatius*. Since I spent twenty years in the religious community he founded, I became familiar with this short but powerful handbook. He introduces, among other types of prayer, forms of guided meditation. One can start with a passage from scripture. Let us consider Acts 2:1–4, a text we referred to earlier in this chapter. "When the day of Pentecost had come, they were all together in one place. And suddenly from heaven there came a sound like the rush of a violent wind, and it filled the entire house where they were sitting. Divided tongues, as of fire, appeared among them, and a tongue rested on each of them. All of them were filled with the Holy Spirit and began to speak in other languages, as the Spirit gave them ability."

Pentecost is the Greek name for the Jewish Feast of *Shavuot* or Weeks, coming fifty (*pente* in Greek) days after Passover. It is a time when Jewish people reflect on their covenantal relationship with God. The disciples are gathered together—men, women, and children—in the house in Jerusalem where they had celebrated Passover on the night before Jesus's crucifixion. It was here, while gathered in prayer, that they had later come to experience Jesus raised from the dead, alive in their hearts and in their fellowship. These intense mystical experiences had bound them together as a community. It was a kind of honeymoon period initially, but now it is over. They realize that Jesus no longer walks among them. His life is now in eternity with God. But he has promised to be with them and to send them his Spirit.

They are pondering this promise while gathered together in prayer, when suddenly there arises in them a great sense of power, as though the Holy Spirit were actually a fire warming their seventh and highest chakra, the top of the head where spiritual bliss and joy are experienced. In this self-guided meditation, you place yourself in this scene. You sit there in prayer with the disciples. You ponder the reality of Jesus's death, his experienced presence in your life after his death, the sobering realization that he has "ascended into heaven," that is, has been removed from the kind of physical presence he had during his teaching ministry.

Sitting there in that upper room, surrounded by Jesus's disciples, including his mother, Mary, you allow yourself to experience the activation of your seventh chakra. You open yourself to the fire of the Spirit, to the Spirit's life and energy, to the Spirit's joy and bliss. You visualize that Spirit as a golden lightfall, cascading down upon you, permeating every fiber of your being, warming and energizing you. You sit quietly, allowing yourself to be receptive to this gift of the Spirit. After awhile, you rise, leave the upper room, and return to the elevator that will bring you back to your world and your Spirit-filled life.

Another beautiful meditation is based on something central in the story of the Buddha. He has just had his dramatic awakening under the tree of enlightenment; he has just overcome myriad temptations to reverse his decision to help others. And now he walks to Deer Park to deliver his first sermon. You are there, sitting with a few other spiritual seekers, anxious to hear what he has to say. He explains the First Noble Truth: Our initial experience of life is unsatisfactory; something is always lacking. He teaches the Second Noble Truth: Reflecting on this unsatisfactory character of life, we realize that its source is not in the nature of the circumstances of our life, but in our wanting things to change that cannot change, our clinging to unreasonable desires instead of recognizing the true nature of what surrounds us.

We then see and hear the Buddha teach the Third Noble Truth: the end of living this frustrated kind of existence. He explains that our very clinging to what is not real is the source of our self-generated suffering. We want reality to conform to our ego needs but such is not the case. And then he reveals the Fourth Noble Truth: the eightfold path to enlightenment. We hear about all the practices we have been considering so far, from right meditation to right behavior, right attention, and right concentration.

You remain there, watching the Buddha, listening to his teaching, hearing the questions and comments of the others who are assembled with you. You let his words soak into the soil of your receptive heart. You let his gentle gaze embrace your being, healing so much that is constricted and painful in your experience of life. And when you are ready, you go up to him and express a particular concern of yours, a question or a plea from the depth of your own being. You listen to what he has to say. And then you say good-bye to him and walk slowly to the elevator that brings you back to your world and the tasks of your day.

Another meditation is embedded in an important day in the life of the prophet Muhammad. You are sitting in a small house in Mecca where he is teaching a group of his followers the message he has been receiving from God. It is a wonderful message—a call to recognize God, to submit one's life to God, and to strive for justice. It stands in strong contrast to the pagan world in Mecca, rife with violence, infanticide toward female children, drunkenness, gambling, the neglect of the poor. You are deeply moved by this man of God, his piercing eyes, his commanding voice. You let the words he is reciting nurture your spiritual hunger.

The quiet scene is disturbed by noises outside the house. Angry voices are protesting this gathering of believers. The people of Mecca do not want to think about the poor, to be kind to their wives, to give up their drunkenness and their gambling. Rocks hit the small house where you are sitting. The prophet of God announces that the community of believers can no longer remain in Mecca. Word has come from the beautiful oasis world of Yahtrib (later to be known as Medina), more than three hundred miles to the north, that a community of believers is there to welcome Muhammad and his message. Soon it will be time to make this flight. The year is 622 C.E.

You approach Muhammad. His loving and peaceful presence enfolds you. You fear the hostile people outside but you are confident that his message of justice and peace is indeed from God. You tell him that you are willing to make this journey with him, if he will take you. He smiles and says that your presence would enrich the community of faith. He lays his hand on your shoulder, assuring you that God will give you the courage you need. He bids you now to go home and prepare yourself for the journey, a journey of faith into an unknown world, much like the one made by the great prophet Abraham so many years ago, when he left Ur to travel where God was leading him. You say good-bye to Muhammad, leave the house, making your way through the angry crowd outside, and you slowly walk to the elevator that will bring you back to your world and the journey of faith stretching before you there.

Reflections

1. Do people see me as hard-hearted? If so, in what circumstances?
2. How might I grow in meekness, mildness, and humility? Does it mean having less ego? less absorption in my own agenda? less confidence in my ability to do without others?
3. How will I notice when my heart is softening?

14

Experiencing God's Reign

THE PROCLAMATION OF GOD'S REIGN BRINGS US TO THE HEART OF JESUS'S message. This chapter, therefore, attempts to understand the mystery of God's reign so central in the life and prayer of a Thomas Believer. What is this kingdom or reign of God that Jesus proclaims? Where is it? Is it here or is it yet to come? Is it within us or does it lie outside of us? Is it in some other place? Is it in some other time? Who brings it? What brings it? Fortunately, we have a number of sayings that speak of God's reign.

> **3a Jesus said: If your leaders say to you "Look! The Kingdom is in the sky!" Then the birds will be there before you are. If they say that the Kingdom is in the sea, then the fish will be there before you are. Rather, the Kingdom is within you and it is outside of you.**

There is humor in this saying. One can imagine Jesus looking up at the clouds in mock anticipation and then (especially if he were teaching by the Sea of Galilee) looking down into the water with feigned curiosity. How many Christians make these same gestures, but without Jesus's sense of humor. Millions of Christians expect to see Jesus coming on the clouds of heaven. If that were to happen, then the birds would prove to be the best Christians. I don't know of any Christian sects anticipating Jesus's Second Coming from the sea; but if that were the case, the fish would be the best Christians. No one is coming on the clouds. No one is coming on the waves. These are images, except to those who have no understanding of religious language and metaphor.

With extraordinary insight, Jesus tells us that the kingdom is both within and outside of us. In the Lord's Prayer, Christians say, "Thy kingdom come. Thy will be done, on earth as it is in heaven." Hebrew poetry is characterized by parallelism, so this is really one petition. May your reign come! And how does God's reign come? When God's will is done on earth as it is at the "heaven" level of consciousness, where the divine mystery dwells most fully. This idea of realizing God's reign on earth is what I was referring to when I wrote about having "hands to make it happen" in the Prelude at the beginning of this book. So we "find" God's reign in the doing of God's will. But what is God's will?

One Jewish response comes from Micah 6:8—"God has told you, O mortal, what is good; and what does the Lord require of you but to do justice, and to love kindness, and to walk humbly with your God?" When Jesus was asked which commandments were the greatest, he responded (Mark 12:28–34): "The first is, 'Hear, O Israel: the Lord our God, the Lord is one; you shall love the Lord your God with all your heart, and with all your soul, and with all your mind, and with all your strength.' The second is this, 'You shall love your neighbor as yourself.' There is no other commandment greater than these." There is a similar statement of Jesus's second commandment attributed to Muhammad: "None among you will be a true believer until he loves for his brother that which he loves for himself."[24]

The convergence of wisdom in the three religions of Abraham gives us clarity about God's will for the world. First, that we recognize God. This entails turning aside from our culture of distraction and denial when the Divine (the numinous) nods at us. Second, that we submit to God (submission is the meaning of *Islam*; a Muslim is one who submits). Third, that we strive for a world of justice. And this "striving for justice" is the true and deepest meaning of the misunderstood concept of *jihad* in Islam. This justice is not an abstraction, the subject of a prolonged discussion of the type we find in Plato's *Republic*. It entails concrete, moment-to-moment concern for our neighbor.

The message and ministry of Jesus emphasize the importance of loving precisely that neighbor who falls outside society's norms. Women were the most marginalized group in Jesus's world, and his words and actions demonstrated a special concern for them. The same was true of the poor, the children, the diseased, the prostitutes, and the hated tax collectors. One of Jesus's boldest parables declares that, at the final judgment, we will all be judged by what we have or have not done "for the least of our brothers and sisters" (Matthew 25:45).

> **8 And he said: The man is like a thoughtful fisherman who threw his net into the sea and pulled it out full of little fish. Among all the little fish, that thoughtful fisherman found one fine large fish that would be beneficial to him and, throwing all the little fish back into the sea, he easily chose to keep the large one. Whoever has ears to hear let him hear.**

So much of the spiritual life involves discernment. What is it that we really want? Oscar Wilde wrote that the worst thing in life is not getting what you want, but the second worst thing is getting it. What is it that we really want? Money, health, our own happiness and the happiness of our loved ones, success, fame, power, or prestige?

When we look at a net full of fish, it's relatively easy to distinguish a big one from a bunch of little ones. But it's not so easy in the net of our lives to discern what really calls for little of our attention and what demands our soul's dedication. For Jesus, the "big fish" is God's reign or kingdom. Everything else becomes inconsequential in comparison to that. This is a teaching that can easily cause us some discomfort, since we don't like to admit how much energy we sometimes put into some very small fish.

> **20 The disciples said to Jesus: Tell us what the Kingdom of Heaven is like. He replied: It is like a mustard seed, the smallest of all. However, when it falls into worked ground it sends out a large stem, and it becomes a shelter for the birds of heaven.**

The beginnings of greatness are often quite small. This mustard seed is common, something found even in the poorest home. It comes from a plant that grows like a weed. And yet, when it is full grown, birds can sometimes find shelter there. How small is the beginning of the spiritual life in us. Sometimes it is a matter of only one glance we cast in the direction of the divine mystery nodding to us in that moment of grace.

Ignatius of Loyola remarked once that even one verse of scripture, if properly assimilated, was enough to make one a saint. He allegedly converted the brilliant Francis Xavier merely by quoting to him one verse of scripture, "What does it profit a human being to gain the whole world if he loses his very essence?" (Mark 8:36). The beginning of God's reign is anything that awakens us from our unconscious acceptance of our societally defined world, the drug to which we are most addicted.

Practice

In a meditation from *The Spiritual Exercises of St. Ignatius* called "The Contemplation to Attain the Love of God," Ignatius asks us to be aware of God working in the world: "Reflect how God dwells in creatures: in the elements giving them existence, in the plants giving them life, in the animals conferring upon them sensation, in man bestowing understanding."[25] He goes on to speak of God dwelling in us, as God's temples, created in God's image and likeness.

Later in this meditation, Ignatius speaks of God working and laboring in all the creatures on the face of the earth. He speaks explicitly of God as "one who labors" in the elements, the animals, the plants where God gives being, conferring life and sensation.[26] We can let our imaginations range over the face of the earth, contemplating the divine reality working in every molecule, every plant and animal, every human being. This can be a helpful practice for experiencing God's reign. Try sitting in your meditation space and using this form of imaginative prayer.

Reflections

1. Do I still think of God's reign as something coming in the future on the clouds of heaven? Or do I find myself more open to understanding God's reign in the here and now of my experience?
2. Can I learn to look for God's reign in the tiniest things that surround me—little snowflakes, drops of water, the smallest of flowers?
3. Can I relax into the experience of God's reign as I seek to do God's will in the world—seeking justice, dialogue, and peace?

15

God's Reign Calls for Ready Hands

> 96 Jesus said: The Kingdom of the Father is like a woman who took a little leaven and concealed it in dough. She made large loaves of bread. He who has ears let him hear.

BREAD DOESN'T COME INTO EXISTENCE MERELY BECAUSE THE YEAST AND dough are lying side by side on the table. Someone has to mix the two together and form the mixture into loaves. God's reign is the result of a twofold action: the woman baking the bread and the elements involved in the process. *Concealed* seems an odd choice of verb, but it picks up on yet another element of the process, the fact that the growth is often hidden. It does not constitute front-page news.

> 97 Jesus said: The Kingdom of the Father is like a woman who was carrying a jar full of grain. As she walked along a handle of her jar broke off and grain trickled out, but she didn't notice. When she arrived in her house, she put the jar down and found it empty.

This parable is not found in the gospels of the Christian Testament. Again, as in the parable of the yeast, the reign of God is compared to a woman. But the story takes a strange twist when the handle of her jar breaks off. The grain begins to disappear from the jar she is carrying. Why doesn't she notice the jar getting lighter? Why doesn't she hear the trickle of grain falling on the path behind her? Her inattentiveness is much like our own. It is the forgetfulness of which Muslims speak, the sleepwalking state of countless Buddhist tales. It is human nature in its untransformed condition.

Both on the personal level and on the larger scale of our society, the grain falls unnoticed from our jars. God's reign slips away from us as we become enamored of the trinkets of our socialized reality, as we buy new cars, designer clothes, and high-tech toys. We convince ourselves that we have no time for an inner life, that the very notion of a spiritual life is a delusion, that matter and power are all that is real. And we pop more pills—to stay awake, to fall asleep, to feel sexual, to feel nothing at all, to sugarcoat the bilious taste of despair in our mouths, to cosmeticize the deathly pallor of our souls.

We experience the larger world with the same lack of awareness that characterizes our personal lives. We shop in glitzy malls, oblivious to the sweatshops that support them, the poor workers living in virtual slavery to produce our luxuries, the victims of our new brand of colonialism. In one of the television interviews following the Oscar nominations, a woman commented on her jewel-studded shoes, mentioning that they were worth a million dollars. The next day, one of my international students asked me how I thought that interview would have been heard in a village where people were still waiting for clean drinking water. And yet, we sit in blissful ignorance in our five-star restaurants, sipping our martinis and wondering why the world hates us.

The president of the United States talks about the whole world someday enjoying our way of life—and no one laughs. Are people so naïve that they don't realize that there aren't sufficient resources to support our way of life for more than a small minority of the planet's population? Does no one reckon the cost of maintaining an empire? That tab far exceeds the billion dollars a day we spend to maintain our military hegemony in the world. It translates into countless Americans living without health care, losing their jobs, struggling to be educated in woefully inadequate schools, coping with despair in our forgotten slums. Our jars are almost empty. Most of God's reign has leaked out of our personal and national life. And we remain as unaware as the woman carelessly walking home.

> **98 Jesus said: The Kingdom of the Father is like a man who intended to kill a powerful man. He drew out his sword in his own house and stabbed it into the wall to test his strength. Then he killed the powerful man.**

It's not strange that the canonical gospels omit this story. It's a disturbing example, suggesting that Jesus was not in favor of peace at any price. Who would such a "powerful man" be to Jesus's listeners? Perhaps a Roman officer attached to the cruel occupation troops of Caesar. Perhaps a greedy landowner engaged in profiting from the misery of his hired workers. The peasants who heard Jesus certainly knew what he meant. And yet, he was not advocating violence against these oppressors. As always in his parables, he was using an experience close to his listeners' hearts to open up the door to a higher teaching and message.

But what precisely is that message? To know God's reign must we kill a powerful person? Who would that be? There are many candidates. It could be our own ego. The ego is such a powerful entity that spiritual wisdom tells us it dies just a few minutes after we do. Is the powerful person the socialized world that exercises such a hypnotic influence over most of us? That too is not an easy person to kill. Is the powerful person the Devil? In that case, this may refer to the exorcisms that often accompany the healing ministries of Jesus and his disciples. Is the powerful person the arrogance of empire that many Jews absorbed from the occupation forces of Rome and that many of us absorb from our current military presence in so many countries of the globe? The answer could be all of the above.

109 Jesus said: The Kingdom is like a man with a treasure of which he is unaware hidden in his field. He died and left the field to his son. His son knew nothing about it and, having received the field, sold it. The new owner came and, while plowing, found the treasure. He began to lend money at interest to anybody he wished.

The treasure in the field seems much like the big fish in the thoughtful fisherman's net. But this parable adds the element of unawareness we saw in the story of the woman with the leaking jar of grain. Both father and son literally don't know what's in their backyard. They live on the surface of life. The new owner plows the field and it is only then that he finds the treasure. We too have to dig beneath the surface to find the treasure. We have to plow the field. We have to disturb what is superficial to discover what is deep. Like the woman making bread, we have to do some work to become aware of the mystery of God's reign.

113 His disciples asked him: When is the Kingdom coming? He replied: It is not coming in an easily observable manner. People will not be saying, "Look, it's over here" or "Look, it's over there." Rather, the Kingdom of the Father is already spread out on the earth, and people aren't aware of it.

This is very appropriate as the last saying in the Gospel of Thomas, considering saying 114 as probably spurious. We are challenged one final time to abandon our stubborn effort to place God's reign somewhere else or at some other time. It can't be here; it must be over there. It can't be now; it must be later. I may go to a monastery in Tibet someday; then I could meditate. Maybe I will volunteer to work with the dying people in Calcutta someday; then I could be so compassionate. If only I can be among those taken up in "the rapture" when Jesus comes, then I will be saved. As individuals and as societies, in our theologies and in our secular ideologies, we multiply ways to avoid "what is already spread out over the earth." We submerge ourselves in distractions so that we can remain among those who "aren't aware of it."

In saying 113 we are dramatically brought back to the theme of presence and awareness. It's spread out on the earth, but we don't see it. It's right now, but we're not in that now. Some are—the poets, the mystics, the saints, those who are becoming Jesus's twins. And that, of course, is the real goal of the Thomas Believer: to experience in this place and at this time the kingdom that can only be known in the here and now.

Let's try to clear up some of the misunderstandings about prayer that have plagued many of us along our way. First of all, we are not praying to an entity who lives somewhere far away from us. The Qur'an tells us that God is as close as our jugular vein. When we address God in prayer, we are addressing the divine mystery that is within us and everyone and everything, the very being of being itself.

And yet, although God is not a separate entity in the universe, God is also not an impersonal energy or life-force but the living God. This is a God we can love, whereas we cannot love the battery charging our car. I remember sitting in a fast-food restaurant in St. Louis, after visiting my father at the nursing home. I was on my way to the airport and my flight home to Chicago. As I sat by the window waiting for my food, time stopped and my heart was filled with a feeling of intense love for God. I sat there for a few minutes, enjoying a consciousness totally transformed. Gradually, I returned to ordinary consciousness and the waiter brought my meal.

William James in his classic *The Varieties of Religious Experience* gives the four characteristics of such experiences, all of which were true of my own. He says that they are ineffable, passive, transient, and noetic.[27] Something is "ineffable" because it cannot be expressed in ordinary dualistic language. That is why poets and mystics speak in metaphors, but even these only suggest the higher consciousness, rather than describing it. I can talk about that day and even wrote a poem about it, but I know that my words can never fathom that experience.

My experience that day was "passive" in the sense that I was aware of something happening to me, not something that I was consciously doing or making happen. It was, alas, all too "transient," though the greatest adepts, avatars, and teachers—like Jesus, Buddha, Krishna, Moses, and Muhammad—inhabit this level of consciousness all the time. Finally, it was "noetic," meaning that it had a knowing component. There was something I learned that day, something I will know all the days of my life.

I want to add a reflection on that third characteristic of mystical experience—its transience. It does not totally disappear. The Hindus cite the example of monks using dye to give their robes a rich ochre color. The cloth can absorb only so much dye at one time. So after the robes dry on the line, they return them to the vat of dye and immerse them once again. Each time this happens, the robe retains a little more of the rich color. I think the same is true of our consciousness. Even today I retain some of the color of that distant day in St. Louis. This is important as we engage in spiritual practice. The meditation continues to affect us, even when the formal time we have dedicated to it is over. This deepening of consciousness is one of the fruits of spiritual practice.

We do not need to cajole or bribe God to love us or care for us. God loves us more than we can love ourselves. God is the very love of our being that causes us to be at all, to exist—literally to stand out (*ex* plus *sto*) from nothingness. This means that a great deal of our prayer should be praise and thanks, not only petition.

Praise seems foreign to some people. Is God some kind of despot needing us to praise the divine mystery? It's not that God needs it; we need it. We need to remind ourselves that what is most important in us and in our world transcends our ego and the corporate egos of our societies. As Rabbi Abraham Joshua Heschel often reminded his students: God is either of supreme importance or of no importance.

And thanks? Perhaps this is the most important characteristic of the spiritual life. Thanks is the opposite of the spirit of complaint. And complaint is the lifeblood of a person or society that is spirit-less. By complaint I don't mean constructive criticism; I mean rather that nagging sense that what is at hand is never enough. It really comes down to the Buddhist awareness of the unsatisfactory character of existence. And it's only when we transcend our ego needs that we can see the adequacy of what is at hand. This is not an invitation to complacency. That adequacy is not an invitation to walk away but to respond.

I learned this lesson from one of my students. He was on our sailing team. He told me one day, after we had studied some of the basic insights of Buddhism, that the teachings reminded him of how to be a good sailor. "A good sailor," he said, "does not complain about the winds. The winds are what they are. The good sailor is the one who knows how to trim the sails to fit the wind, how to use the wind to sail his boat." Life is much like that. One who lives well doesn't spend a lot of time complaining about the circumstances at hand; circumstances are the stuff out of which we make our lives. The quality of the lives we make lies in the skill of our hands, not in the nature of the circumstances. As a Buddhist friend of mine often says, "This moment is adequate for practice." So we need to say "thank you" and get on with it.

What are we asking for when we ask for things? It depends on the level of our development. I remember a little boy at a First Communion; it was taking place as a "home Mass" with a small community celebrating this event in the family's living room. At one point in the service, the little boy prayed that God would send jellybeans down on everyone there. When his mother asked him if he could think of anything better to pray for, he paused for a moment and said, "No." If jellybeans seem like the best thing to ask for, then ask for jellybeans. But a time comes when most of us get beyond jellybeans. But do we really? Ultimately, all of our petitions are for jellybeans until we learn to pray only for God, for God's Spirit, and for God's will. But we don't have to jump to that with one giant step. We need to take the step ahead of us. We do need to be ready, however, when it's time to stop praying for jellybeans.

I remember a conversation with one of my Jesuit scholastic (seminarian) teachers when I was in high school. We had been singing a hymn at Mass, based on a prayer of Ignatius in *The Spiritual Exercises of St. Ignatius*. It's a prayer known to practitioners of Ignatian spirituality as "Take, Lord, and Receive." The hymn (as close as I can remember it) ended with the phrase "Give me only your love and your grace and I'll not ask for anything more." I told the young Jesuit teacher that I didn't think I could really make that prayer my own. There was a lot more I wanted to ask for at the age of seventeen. I still find myself asking for a lot more—though at the deepest level, there really is nothing more to ask for than God's love and grace.

The wise young teacher first of all congratulated me for paying attention to the words of the hymn at all, as well as for my honesty, and then told me to keep praying for all the things I wanted but to keep this prayer in mind as a goal in my spiritual life. He promised that it would eventually purify my prayers of petition. Perhaps God is granting me a long life so that I will eventually be able to pray that prayer of Ignatius, even if it is my deathbed prayer.

Practice

Ignatius of Loyola suggests a method of prayer in which you say one word with each breath. I have done this with groups of people and it has a calming effect. You can do this with any prayer of your choice. I will illustrate it here with a prayer central to my own practice, a prayer that Jesus taught his disciples (Matthew 6:9–13). You can sit in the meditation position and say this prayer (or any other prayer) in this way.

"Heavenly [breath] Parent [breath], may [breath] your [breath] Name [breath] be [breath] holy [breath]." Continue in this manner with the rest of the prayer: "May your reign come on earth as in heaven. Give us today our bread for the coming day. Forgive us our failings as we forgive those who fail us. Let us not fall when we are tested but deliver us from all evil. Amen." Saying the prayer this way takes about three minutes. Sometimes, however, a word will strike you and you may want to stay with it for a while. One can easily end up spending a full fifteen or twenty minutes with this method of prayer. Try this method with any other prayer or hymn or sacred poem you know and love.

Prayer is a many-faceted reality and exploring it takes us all the days of our life. It is our highest human activity. Plants at their highest level of evolution seem to want to be animals. We think, for example, of the plants that catch flies and other insects. We had one at the high school where I taught, but it died from too much hamburger. Animals, on the other hand, seem to want to be humans. Anyone with a pet knows that these animals sometimes look at us as though they were on the verge of speech. What are we humans doing, then, when we are at our limit and are standing on tiptoe, striving for the next level of our own spiritual evolution? We are praying.

Reflections

1. Does prayer still seem to conjure up for me a universe in which God is an old man on a cloud listening to me?
2. Can I begin to think of prayer as addressing that divine center that is at the core of all that is, myself as well as others?
3. How can I be a more prayerful person while still being true to my understanding of the spiritual universe?

16

Spirituality Is Not Skygazing

11a Jesus said: This sky will cease to be, and the sky above it will cease to be.

SAYING 11A IS CHALLENGING. THE IDEA OF MANY LEVELS OF HEAVEN WAS common at this time. Jesus is here asserting that eventually both the first heaven (presumably the sky) and the second heaven (perhaps the realm of the manifested light of the first day of creation) will disappear. In other words, God as manifested will one day cease to be and only the Unmanifest will exist.

11b The dead do not live, and the living will not die.

Saying 1 encouraged us to correctly interpret these sayings, because then we will never die. If we attain true life, we will never die. In other words, if we achieve the level of unity consciousness in which we experience our oneness with the One, then we have attained a life that death cannot destroy. On the other hand, if we stay with dead things—the empty rituals and observances of exoteric religion—we ourselves are dead and there is nothing in us to bring us to life.

11c When you ate dead things, you made them alive. When you arrive into light, what will you do?

The first sentence is fairly easy to understand. Our normal diet consists of things that are dead—animals, plants, fruits, and vegetables—and yet our bodies are able to assimilate these dead things and through them nurture our physical life. With that ordinary awareness as background, we are then asked the challenging question: What will we do when we arrive into light?

First of all, does this mean something that happens in life or after death, or both? We arrive into light when our higher chakras are activated, when higher levels of consciousness are reached. We also arrive into light when we pass into the next phase of our existence after our physical death. What indeed will we do in either of these situations? Will we eat living things instead of the dead things we eat now? God's Word is a living thing; perhaps we will be nurtured solely by God's Word, God's light, God's life. The ancient Greeks posited that the gods ate *ambrosia,* literally, "not bread." When Jesus is tempted by Satan to turn stones into bread (Matthew 4:4), he quotes Deuteronomy 8:3, "People cannot live on bread alone but on every word that comes from the mouth of the Lord."

11d When you were one, you became two. When you become two, what will you do?

We return now to the theme of oneness and duality. Davies sees this as the original division of the one human being into two (Adam and Eve) and our efforts now to re-create that mythic time when we were one.[28] This fits with all the teachings relating to this business of making the two one again; that is, reaching a consciousness that transcends the duality of ordinary life and ordinary religion.

This dualistic thinking constitutes one of the chief differences between Thomas Believers and the faithful of most religions. Consider this in terms of the belief of most Roman Catholics, the world's largest Christian denomination. We are here and God is up there. We are mere humans but Jesus is God. We are sinners but Jesus redeems us. Our works are useless but grace saves us. Sex is dirty but celibacy is holy. We are children but the priest is "Father" and the pope is "the

Holy Father." Our homes, schools, and workplaces are part of the profane world (the word *profane* literally means "in front of the temple") but the sanctuary of our church is a holy space. Reality is secular but religion is holy.

Thomas Believers reject this dualistic way of thinking. It's not that Thomas Believers have no clergy; they have no laity. There is neither a God out there nor a distant Redeemer. Lovemaking is no less holy than the kiss of peace in church. The food we share at our tables is as God-filled as Holy Communion. For Thomas Believers, God created reality, but human beings created religion. The place where you are standing is as holy as any sanctuary. Thomas Believers seek to live from a consciousness of a restored unity, even though most of the world still lives in a consciousness of division.

> **18a The disciples asked Jesus: Tell us about our end. What will it be? Jesus replied: Have you found the Beginning so that you now seek the end? The place of the Beginning will be the place of the end.**

In mythic description, the end often replicates the beginning. The biblical descriptions of the end time, with their visions of peace and prosperity, hark back to the garden from which our first parents were driven. All reality comes from the One and returns to the One. Our goal is always to reach the place of our beginning. The difference, of course, is that at the end we truly understand it, whereas at the beginning it was simply and unconsciously there. The children whom Jesus frequently praises are not aware of what adults realize when they rediscover the pure child of God within their own hearts.

> **38 Jesus said: You often wanted to hear the words I am speaking to you. You have no one else from whom you can hear them. The days will come when you will seek me and you will not be able to find me.**

We "often wanted" to hear the words Jesus is speaking. That's in the past. Are we, then, listening to those words now? Or are we putting the challenge to spiritual growth that Jesus represents off to some distant future? How do we know that we will have that future opportunity if we are not taking advantage of this present one? The injunction to live neither in the future nor in the past but solely in the present is a constant theme in these teachings.

> **52 His disciples said to him: Twenty-four prophets spoke to Israel, and they all spoke of you. He responded to them: You have deserted the living one who is with you, and you spoke about the dead.**

This teaching strikes at the heart of so much of what passes for religion today. Watch the televangelists and you will see them pulling up isolated proof texts from scripture to demonstrate their particular belief system. But isn't all of this activity no more than unearthing skeletons in a graveyard? Jesus contrasts "the living one who is with you" with "the dead." Is our religiosity nothing but a stirring around of old bones? Or are we in touch with anything alive, vibrant, and speaking in us now? No wonder so many religious services are boring. The clergy are merely muttering in dusty museums. No breath of life is there.

> **51 His disciples asked him: When will the dead rest? When will the new world arrive? He replied: That which you are waiting for has come, but you don't recognize it.**

The entire enterprise contained in these teachings is located not in time, but in consciousness (recognition). The essential mistake of religion, certainly of organized Christianity, has been to make temporal and spatial distinctions instead of consciousness ones. Nothing is "up there" or "down there"; nothing is "coming on the clouds of heaven." What we need is not more reality but more recognition.

Practice

How do you think of awareness? I think of it sometimes like a miner's flashlight strapped to your forehead. The light of awareness is always on. Every time we realize that we are aware, we are learning awareness. Every time we realize that we are not aware, we are learning awareness. This awareness is the soil in which all of our practice grows.

When we do noncognitive meditation, we are basking in pure awareness. We are aware of sounds that enter our silent space, of distractions that flow through our minds, of feelings and sensations that appear suddenly on the computer screen of our mind. We don't need to deal with any of this during the meditation. We simply need to be aware.

When we practice repetition, awareness suffuses the practice. The words work with the rhythm of our lives. Usually, when I wake up in the morning, the repetition just begins on its own. When I first become aware of the words used in my repetition practice, they are already moving in my mind and heart. They continue throughout the day, whenever I am not consciously directing my attention to some other task. The repetition practice helps to ground me in the here and now.

Our practice of guided meditation also flows from awareness. We move in our imagination to a quiet space where we meet our guide, asking advice and help for the day stretching out before us. We read a sacred text and find a story that we can enter in our imagination, moving around in the scene and feeling it as one who is there. The present is always our focus. What is the guide telling me now? What is my participation in this scene disclosing to me now?

Prayer lives totally in awareness. We say a prayer we know by heart, repeating one word with each breath. We talk spontaneously to the divine reality within us. We praise or thank the God Who Is. We ask for help or healing for ourselves and those we love and those we find it hard to love. We abide in the divine mystery, whether in silence, song, or speech. Prayer becomes our home, our monastic cell where we are always alone with the Only One. A monastic admonition states that a monastic should rarely leave her cell, but when she does leave her cell, she should take it with her. So the cell is not the physical space but the place of consciousness and awareness, the soul's home.

When we do bodily practice, let that awareness illuminate the sensations in our body. At the gym this morning, I tried to be aware of the feelings in each muscle group I was exercising. When I first started at the gym, I asked my trainer how I could learn what muscle group each exercise is affecting. He looked at me somewhat startled and said, "Those will be the ones you feel during the exercise." A typical academic, I wanted to start from a definition instead of from the experience itself.

Our practice of generosity flows from awareness. We don't have to set up a plan for ten generous deeds per day. When the occasion arises, the act appears. It all happens so spontaneously that it occurs before our left hand knows what our right hand is doing. These deeds are always in the present, so the more that present moment is illuminated by awareness, the more richly textured our generous deeds can be. When our awareness lessens, so too does our capacity to be generous.

Now the state of mind achieved in these practices is called *contemplatio* (contemplation) in the tradition of the Christian West. This is not itself a practice but the fruit of practice. In these sayings in the Gospel of Thomas, contemplation corresponds to what is called "rest." This is something only one who is spiritually adult (and, therefore, spiritually a child) can experience. It constitutes a climate of the soul that one can know only when one has learned to be alone, *monachos*. And it is only when one knows how to be alone that one is fit to be with others and experience community.

Reflections

1. What do I think of when I hear that someone is "a contemplative"? Does this conjure up images of monastic cells and bread and water fasts?
2. Can I see contemplation as the real goal of all the practices we have been studying?
3. Can I see contemplation as the natural counterpart to true action, so that I realize that the one who acts for justice is a contemplative in action, just as the true contemplative is a justice seeker at prayer?

NOTES

1. I am using the translation by Stevan Davies in the SkyLight Illuminations Series, *The Gospel of Thomas: Annotated and Explained* (Woodstock, Vt., SkyLight Paths, 2002).
2. Alan Race's book is *Christians and Religious Pluralism: Patterns in the Christian Theology of Religions* (London: SCM Press, 1993). Diana Eck's book is *Encountering God: A Spiritual Journey from Bozeman to Banaras*, 2nd ed. (Boston: Beacon Press, 2003).
3. In reading Karen King, I came to see that she shares the same conclusion I had reached through my own studies. She states, on p. 155 of *The Gospel of Mary of Magdala: Jesus and the First Woman Apostle* (Santa Rosa, Calif.: Polebridge Press, 2003), "But there was no religion in antiquity called Gnosticism. Scholars invented the term in the process of categorizing the variety of early Christian heresies."
4. If you want to examine the puerile theology behind their novels, you can read *Are We Living in the End Times?* by Tim LaHaye and Jerry B. Jenkins (Wheaton, Ill.: Tyndale House Publishers, 1999). What is both tragic and amazing, of course, is that these novels are best sellers. This offers dramatic proof of the desire of most people to flee from the demands of the here and now, escaping into a never-never land of fairy tale and fantasy.

5. Davies, p. 74.
6. I am using as a source *The Message of the Qur'an* translated and explained by Muhammad Asad (Gibraltar: Dar Al-Andalus, 1980). This is an excellent translation with abundant footnotes.
7. This excellent book (Berkeley, Calif.: Berkeley Hills Books, 2001) won the American Book Award in 2002.
8. Davies, p. 32.
9. See any of Elaine Pagels's books, but especially her recent *Beyond Belief: The Secret Gospel of Thomas* (New York: Random House, 2003).
10. This is a saying attributed to Shimon the Righteous. In a contemporary reading, Rabbi Rami Shapiro translates this as: "The world stands upon three things—Upon Reality, Upon self-emptying prayer and meditation, Upon acts of love and kindness," in *Wisdom of the Jewish Sages: A Modern Reading of Pirke Avot* (New York: Bell Tower, 1995), p. 3.
11. Assad Nimer Busool, *The Bouquet of the Noble Hadith* (Chicago: The Qur'an Society, 1998), p. 31.
12. Shapiro, p. 6.
13. This can be found in Andrew Harvey, ed., *Teachings of Rumi* (Boston: Shambhala, 1999), p. 142.
14. I discuss these thinkers and their contributions to my own sense of spirituality at greater length in an essay I wrote, entitled "Space for Spirit," in *Finding a Way: Essays on Spiritual Practice*, edited by Lorette Zirker (Boston: C. E. Tuttle, 1996).
15. W. H. Gardner, ed., *Poems and Prose of Gerard Manley Hopkins* (Harmondsworth, Middlesex, UK: Penguin Books, 1953), p. 82.
16. I am very much indebted to my colleague and friend Rabbi Rami Shapiro for his insights in this whole area of principles of practice. I would especially recommend his book *Minyan: Ten Principles for Living a Life of Integrity* (New York: Bell Tower, 1997), for a more in-depth discussion of several of the practices I have chosen to incorporate in this book.

17. Anselm (1033–1109) put this doctrine forward in a classic text called *Cur Deus Homo* ("Why God Became Man"). You can find it in most Anselm anthologies, for example, in *St. Anselm: Basic Writings*, 2nd ed. (LaSalle, Ill.: Open Court Publishing Company, 1988).
18. James Carroll, *Constantine's Sword: The Church and the Jews* (Boston: Houghton Mifflin Company, 2001).
19. Busool, p. 14.
20. See his *The Gospel According to Jesus: A New Translation and Guide to His Essential Teaching for Believers* (New York: HarperCollins, 1991).
21. Jane Schaberg, *The Illegitimacy of Jesus: A Feminist Theological Interpretation of the Infancy Narratives* (San Francisco: Harper & Row, 1987).
22. Busool, p. 19.
23. Davies, p. 92.
24. Busool, p. 12.
25. Louis J. Puhl, S.J., trans. *The Spiritual Exercises of St. Ignatius: Based on Studies in the Language of the Autograph* (Chicago: Loyola University Press, 1952), p. 102.
26. Ibid., p. 103.
27. Originally given as the prestigious Gifford Lectures in Edinburgh, Scotland, this book by James was first published in 1902. This passage occurs in the chapter on mysticism, the most remarkable in the book. I would certainly consider this to be the most influential book on religion by an American in the twentieth century.
28. Davies, p. 12.

SELECT BIBLIOGRAPHY

Asad, Muhammad. *The Message of the Qur'an.* Gibraltar: Dar Al-Andalus, 1980.

Borg, Marcus J. *The Heart of Christianity: Rediscovering a Life of Faith.* San Francisco: HarperSanFrancisco, 2003.

Busool, Assad Nimer. *The Bouquet of the Noble Hadith.* Chicago: The Qur'an Society, 1998.

Dart, John, and Ray Riegert. *The Gospel of Thomas: Unearthing the Lost Words of Jesus.* Berkeley, Calif.: Ulysses Press, 2000.

Davies, Stevan, trans. and ed. *The Gospel of Thomas: Annotated and Explained.* Woodstock, Vt.: SkyLight Paths, 2002.

Fox, Matthew. *The Coming of the Cosmic Christ: The Healing of Mother Earth and the Birth of a Global Renaissance.* San Francisco: Harper & Row, 1988.

Ignatius of Loyola. *The Spiritual Exercises of St. Ignatius: Based on Studies in the Language of the Autograph.* Translated by Louis J. Puhl, S. J. Chicago: Loyola University Press, 1952.

King, Karen. *The Gospel of Mary of Magdala: Jesus and the First Woman Apostle.* Santa Rosa, Calif.: Polebridge Press, 2003.

Miller, Ron. *The Hidden Gospel of Matthew: Annotated and Explained.* Woodstock, Vt.: SkyLight Paths, 2004.

———. *Wisdom of the Carpenter: 365 Prayers and Meditations of Jesus from the Gospel of Thomas, Lost Gospel Q, Secret Book of James, and the New Testament.* Berkeley, Calif.: Ulysses Press, 2003.

Nagler, Michael N. *Is There No Other Way?: The Search for a Nonviolent Future.* Berkeley, Calif.: Berkeley Hills Books, 2001.

Pagels, Elaine. *Beyond Belief: The Secret Gospel of Thomas.* New York: Random House, 2003.

Shapiro, Rami. *Minyan: Ten Principles for Living a Life of Integrity.* New York: Bell Tower, 1997.

Spong, John Shelby. *A New Christianity for a New World: Why Traditional Faith Is Dying and How a New Faith Is Being Born.* San Francisco: HarperSanFrancisco, 2001.

NOTES

About SKYLIGHT PATHS Publishing

SkyLight Paths Publishing is creating a place where people of different spiritual traditions come together for challenge and inspiration, a place where we can help each other understand the mystery that lies at the heart of our existence.

Through spirituality, our religious beliefs are increasingly becoming a part of our lives—rather than *apart* from our lives. While many of us may be more interested than ever in spiritual growth, we may be less firmly planted in traditional religion. Yet, we do want to deepen our relationship to the sacred, to learn from our own as well as from other faith traditions, and to practice in new ways.

SkyLight Paths sees both believers and seekers as a community that increasingly transcends traditional boundaries of religion and denomination—people wanting to learn from each other, *walking together, finding the way.*

We at SkyLight Paths take great care to produce beautiful books that present meaningful spiritual content in a form that reflects the art of making high quality books. Therefore, we want to acknowledge those who contributed to the production of this book.

PRODUCTION
Sara Dismukes & Tim Holtz

EDITORIAL
Sarah McBride, Maura D. Shaw & Emily Wichland

INTERIOR TYPESETTING
Kristin Goble, PerfecType, Nashville, Tennessee

PRINTING & BINDING
Versa Press, East Peoria, Illinois

AVAILABLE FROM BETTER BOOKSTORES.
TRY YOUR BOOKSTORE FIRST.

Spirituality

Journeys of Simplicity: *Traveling Light with Thomas Merton, Bashō, Edward Abbey, Annie Dillard & Others*

by *Philip Harnden*

There is a more graceful way of traveling through life.

Offers vignettes of forty "travelers" and the few ordinary things they carried with them—from place to place, from day to day, from birth to death. What Thoreau took to Walden Pond. What Thomas Merton packed for his final trip to Asia. What Annie Dillard keeps in her writing tent. What an impoverished cook served M. F. K. Fisher for dinner. Much more. "'How much should I carry with me?' is the quintessential question for any journey, especially the journey of life. Herein you'll find sage, sly, wonderfully subversive advice."
—Bill McKibben, author of *The End of Nature* and *Enough*
5 x 7¼, 128 pp, HC, ISBN 1-893361-76-4 **$16.95**

The Alphabet of Paradise: *An A–Z of Spirituality for Everyday Life*

by *Howard Cooper*

"An extraordinary book." —Karen Armstrong

Howard Cooper takes us on a journey of discovery—into ourselves and into the past—to find the signposts that can help us live more meaningful lives. In twenty-six engaging chapters—from A to Z—Cooper spiritually illuminates the subjects of daily life, using an ancient Jewish mystical method of interpretation that reveals both the literal and more allusive meanings of each. Topics include: Awe, Bodies, Creativity, Dreams, Emotions, and more.
5 x 7¾, 224 pp, Quality PB, ISBN 1-893361-80-2 **$16.95**

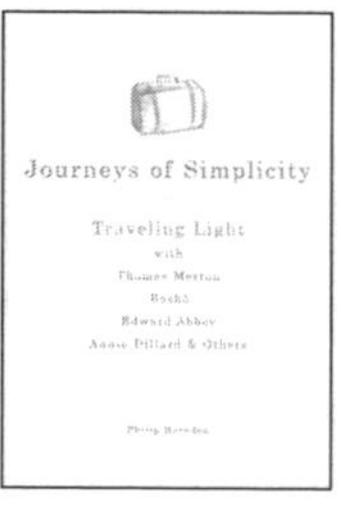

Winter: *A Spiritual Biography of the Season*

Edited by *Gary Schmidt* and *Susan M. Felch;* Illustrations by *Barry Moser*

In thirty stirring pieces, *Winter* delves into the varied feelings that winter conjures in us, calling up both the barrenness and the beauty of the natural world in wintertime. Includes selections by Will Campbell, Rachel Carson, Annie Dillard, Donald Hall, Ron Hansen, Jane Kenyon, Jamaica Kincaid, Barry Lopez, Kathleen Norris, John Updike, E. B. White, and many others. "This outstanding anthology features top-flight nature and spirituality writers on the fierce, inexorable season of winter.... Remarkably lively and warm, despite the icy subject."
—★*Publishers Weekly* Starred Review
6 x 9, 288 pp, 6 b/w illus., Deluxe PB w/flaps, ISBN 1-893361-92-6 **$18.95**
HC, ISBN 1-893361-53-5 **$21.95**

Or phone, fax, mail or e-mail to: SKYLIGHT PATHS **Publishing**
Sunset Farm Offices, Route 4 • P.O. Box 237 • Woodstock, Vermont 05091
Tel: (802) 457-4000 • Fax: (802) 457-4004 • www.skylightpaths.com
Credit card orders: (800) 962-4544 (8:30AM–5:30PM ET Monday–Friday)
Generous discounts on quantity orders. SATISFACTION GUARANTEED. Prices subject to change.

Spiritual Biography

The Life of Evelyn Underhill
An Intimate Portrait of the Groundbreaking Author of Mysticism

by *Margaret Cropper;* Foreword by *Dana Greene*

Evelyn Underhill was a passionate writer and teacher who wrote elegantly on mysticism, worship, and devotional life. This is the story of how she made her way toward spiritual maturity, from her early days of agnosticism to the years when her influence was felt throughout the world. 6 x 9, 288 pp, 5 b/w photos, Quality PB, ISBN 1-893361-70-5 **$18.95**

Zen Effects: *The Life of Alan Watts*

by *Monica Furlong*

The first and only full-length biography of one of the most charismatic spiritual leaders of the twentieth century—now back in print!

Through his widely popular books and lectures, Alan Watts (1915–1973) did more to introduce Eastern philosophy and religion to Western minds than any figure before or since. Here is the only biography of this charismatic figure, who served as Zen teacher, Anglican priest, lecturer, academic, entertainer, a leader of the San Francisco renaissance, and author of more than 30 books, including *The Way of Zen, Psychotherapy East and West* and *The Spirit of Zen.*
6 x 9, 264 pp, Quality PB, ISBN 1-893361-32-2 **$16.95**

Simone Weil: *A Modern Pilgrimage*

by *Robert Coles*

The extraordinary life of the spiritual philosopher who's been called both saint and madwoman.

The French writer and philosopher Simone Weil (1906–1943) devoted her life to a search for God—while avoiding membership in organized religion. Robert Coles' intriguing study of Weil details her short, eventful life, and is an insightful portrait of the beloved and controversial thinker whose life and writings influenced many (from T. S. Eliot to Adrienne Rich to Albert Camus), and continue to inspire seekers everywhere. 6 x 9, 208 pp, Quality PB, ISBN 1-893361-34-9 **$16.95**

Mahatma Gandhi: *His Life and Ideas*

by *Charles F. Andrews;* Foreword by *Dr. Arun Gandhi*

An intimate biography of one of the greatest social and religious reformers of the modern world.

Examines from a contemporary Christian activist's point of view the religious ideas and political dynamics that influenced the birth of the peaceful resistance movement, the primary tool that Gandhi and the people of his homeland would use to gain India its freedom from British rule. An ideal introduction to the life and life's work of this great spiritual leader.
6 x 9, 336 pp, 5 b/w photos, Quality PB, ISBN 1-893361-89-6 **$18.95**

Meditation/Prayer

Finding Grace at the Center: *The Beginning of Centering Prayer*

by *M. Basil Pennington,* OCSO, *Thomas Keating,* OCSO, and *Thomas E. Clarke,* SJ

The book that helped launch the Centering Prayer "movement." Explains the prayer of *The Cloud of Unknowing,* posture and relaxation, the three simple rules of centering prayer, and how to cultivate centering prayer throughout all aspects of your life.

5 x 7¼,112 pp, HC, ISBN 1-893361-69-1 **$14.95**

Prayers to an Evolutionary God

by *William Cleary;* Afterword by *Diarmuid O'Murchu*

How is it possible to pray when God is dislocated from heaven, dispersed all around us, and more of a creative force than an all-knowing father? In this unique collection of eighty prose prayers and related commentary, William Cleary considers new ways of thinking about God and the world around us. Inspired by the spiritual and scientific teachings of Diarmuid O'Murchu and Teilhard de Chardin, Cleary reveals that religion and science can be combined to create an expanding view of the universe—an evolutionary faith.

6 x 9, 208 pp, HC, ISBN 1-59473-006-7 **$21.99**

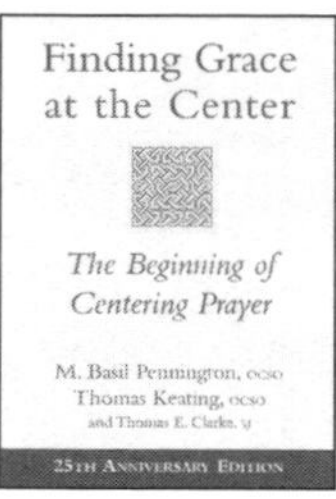

Meditation without Gurus
A Guide to the Heart of Practice

by *Clark Strand*

Short, compelling reflections show you how to make meditation a part of your daily life, without the complication of gurus, mantras, retreats, or treks to distant mountains. This enlightening book strips the practice down to its essential heart—simplicity, lightness, and peace—showing you that the most important part of practice is not whether you can get in the full lotus position, but rather your ability to become fully present in the moment.

5½ x 8½, 192 pp, Quality PB, ISBN 1-893361-93-4 **$16.95**

Meditation & Its Practices
A Definitive Guide to Techniques and Traditions of Meditation in Yoga and Vedanta

by *Swami Adiswarananda*

The complete sourcebook for exploring Hinduism's two most time-honored traditions of meditation.

Drawing on both classic and contemporary sources, this comprehensive sourcebook outlines the scientific, psychological, and spiritual elements of Yoga and Vedanta meditation.

6 x 9, 504 pp, HC, ISBN 1-893361-83-7 **$34.95**

Spiritual Practice

The Sacred Art of Bowing
Preparing to Practice

by *Andi Young*

This informative and inspiring introduction to bowing—and related spiritual practices—shows you how to do it, why it's done, and what spiritual benefits it has to offer. Incorporates interviews, personal stories, illustrations of bowing in practice, advice on how you can incorporate bowing into your daily life, and how bowing can deepen spiritual understanding.
5½ x 8½, 128 pp, b/w illus., Quality PB, ISBN 1-893361-82-9 **$14.95**

Praying with Our Hands: *Twenty-One Practices of Embodied Prayer from the World's Spiritual Traditions*

by *Jon M. Sweeney;* Photographs by *Jennifer J. Wilson;*
Foreword by *Mother Tessa Bielecki;* Afterword by *Taitetsu Unno, PhD*

A spiritual guidebook for bringing prayer into our bodies.

This inspiring book of reflections and accompanying photographs shows us twenty-one simple ways of using our hands to speak to God, to enrich our devotion and ritual. All express the various approaches of the world's religious traditions to bringing the body into worship. Spiritual traditions represented include Anglican, Sufi, Zen, Roman Catholic, Yoga, Shaker, Hindu, Jewish, Pentecostal, Eastern Orthodox, and many others.
8 x 8, 96 pp, 22 duotone photographs, Quality PB, ISBN 1-893361-16-0 **$16.95**

The Sacred Art of Listening
Forty Reflections for Cultivating a Spiritual Practice

by *Kay Lindahl;* Illustrations by *Amy Schnapper*

More than ever before, we need to embrace the skills and practice of listening. You will learn to: Speak clearly from your heart • Communicate with courage and compassion • Heighten your awareness for deep listening • Enhance your ability to listen to people with different belief systems. 8 x 8, 160 pp, Illus., Quality PB, ISBN 1-893361-44-6 **$16.99**

Labyrinths from the Outside In
Walking to Spiritual Insight—A Beginner's Guide

by *Donna Schaper* and *Carole Ann Camp*

The user-friendly, interfaith guide to making and using labyrinths—for meditation, prayer, and celebration.

Labyrinth walking is a spiritual exercise *anyone* can do. This accessible guide unlocks the mysteries of the labyrinth for all of us, providing ideas for using the labyrinth walk for prayer, meditation, and celebrations to mark the most important moments in life. Includes instructions for making a labyrinth of your own and finding one in your area.
6 x 9, 208 pp, b/w illus. and photographs, Quality PB, ISBN 1-893361-18-7 **$16.95**

SkyLight Illuminations Series

Andrew Harvey, series editor

Offers today's spiritual seeker an enjoyable entry into the great classic texts of the world's spiritual traditions. Each classic is presented in an accessible translation, with facing pages of guided commentary from experts, giving you the keys you need to understand the history, context, and meaning of the text. This series enables readers of all backgrounds to experience and understand classic spiritual texts directly, and to make them a part of their lives. Andrew Harvey writes the foreword to each volume, an insightful, personal introduction to each classic.

Bhagavad Gita: *Annotated & Explained*

Translation by *Shri Purohit Swami;* Annotation by *Kendra Crossen Burroughs*

"The very best Gita for first-time readers." —Ken Wilber

Millions of people turn daily to India's most beloved holy book, whose universal appeal has made it popular with non-Hindus and Hindus alike. This edition introduces you to the characters, explains references and philosophical terms, shares the interpretations of famous spiritual leaders and scholars, and more. 5½ x 8½, 192 pp, Quality PB, ISBN 1-893361-28-4 **$16.95**

The Way of a Pilgrim: *Annotated & Explained*

Translation and annotation by *Gleb Pokrovsky*

This classic of Russian spirituality is the delightful account of one man who sets out to learn the prayer of the heart—also known as the "Jesus prayer"—and how the practice transforms his life. 5½ x 8½, 160 pp, Illus., Quality PB, ISBN 1-893361-31-4 **$14.95**

The Gospel of Thomas: *Annotated & Explained*

Translation and annotation by *Stevan Davies*

Discovered in 1945, this collection of aphoristic sayings sheds new light on the origins of Christianity and the intriguing figure of Jesus, portraying the Kingdom of God as a present fact about the world, rather than a future promise or future threat. This edition guides you through the text with annotations that focus on the meaning of the sayings.
5½ x 8½, 192 pp, Quality PB, ISBN 1-893361-45-4 **$16.95**

Rumi and Islam: *Selections from His Stories, Poems, and Discourses—Annotated & Explained*

Translation and annotation by *Ibrahim Gamard*

Offers a new way of thinking about Rumi's poetry. Ibrahim Gamard focuses on Rumi's place within the Sufi tradition of Islam, providing you with insight into the mystical side of the religion—one that has love of God at its core and sublime wisdom teachings as its pathways.
5½ x 8½, 240 pp, Quality PB, ISBN 1-59473-002-4 **$15.99**

SkyLight Illuminations Series

Andrew Harvey, series editor

Zohar: *Annotated & Explained*

Translation and annotation by *Daniel C. Matt*

The cornerstone text of Kabbalah.

The best-selling author of *The Essential Kabbalah* brings together in one place the most important teachings of the *Zohar,* the canonical text of Jewish mystical tradition. Guides you step by step through the midrash, mystical fantasy, and Hebrew scripture that make up the *Zohar,* explaining the inner meanings in facing-page commentary. Ideal for readers without any prior knowledge of Jewish mysticism.

5½ x 8½, 176 pp, Quality PB, ISBN 1-893361-51-9 **$15.99**

Selections from the Gospel of Sri Ramakrishna
Annotated & Explained

Translation by *Swami Nikhilananda;* Annotation by *Kendra Crossen Burroughs*

The words of India's greatest example of God-consciousness and mystical ecstasy in recent history.

Introduces the fascinating world of the Indian mystic and the universal appeal of his message that has inspired millions of devotees for more than a century. Selections from the original text and insightful yet unobtrusive commentary highlight the most important and inspirational teachings. Ideal for readers without any prior knowledge of Hinduism.

5½ x 8½, 240 pp, b/w photographs, Quality PB, ISBN 1-893361-46-2 **$16.95**

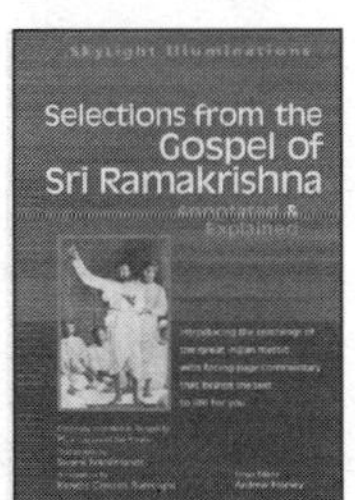

Dhammapada: *Annotated & Explained*

Translation by *Max Müller* and revised by *Jack Maguire;* Annotation by *Jack Maguire*

The classic of Buddhist spiritual practice.

The Dhammapada—words spoken by the Buddha himself over 2,500 years ago—is notoriously difficult to understand for the first-time reader. Now you can experience it with understanding even if you have no previous knowledge of Buddhism. Enlightening facing-page commentary explains all the names, terms, and references, giving you deeper insight into the text.

5½ x 8½, 160 pp, b/w photographs, Quality PB, ISBN 1-893361-42-X **$14.95**

Hasidic Tales: *Annotated & Explained*

Translation and annotation by *Rabbi Rami Shapiro*

The legendary tales of the impassioned Hasidic rabbis.

The allegorical quality of Hasidic tales can be perplexing. Here, they are presented as stories rather than parables, making them accessible and meaningful. Each demonstrates the spiritual power of unabashed joy, offers lessons for leading a holy life, and reminds us that the Divine can be found in the everyday. Annotations explain theological concepts, introduce major characters, and clarify references unfamiliar to most readers.

5½ x 8½, 240 pp, Quality PB, ISBN 1-893361-86-1 **$16.95**

Children's Spirituality

MULTICULTURAL, NONDENOMINATIONAL, NONSECTARIAN

Where Does God Live?

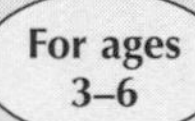

by *August Gold* and *Matthew J. Perlman*

Using simple, everyday examples that children can relate to, this colorful book helps young readers develop a personal understanding of God.

10 x 8½, 32 pp, Quality PB, Full-color photo illus., ISBN 1-893361-39-X **$8.99**

God in Between

For ages 4 & up

by *Sandy Eisenberg Sasso;* Full-color illus. by *Sally Sweetland*

If you wanted to find God, where would you look? A magical, mythical tale that teaches that God can be found where we are: within all of us and the relationships between us. "This happy and wondrous book takes our children on a sweet and holy journey into God's presence." —Rabbi Wayne Dosick, PhD, author of *The Business Bible* and *Soul Judaism*

9 x 12, 32 pp, HC, Full-color illus., ISBN 1-879045-86-9 **$16.95**

Cain & Abel: *Finding the Fruits of Peace*

For ages 5 & up

by *Sandy Eisenberg Sasso;* Full-color illus. by *Joani Keller Rothenberg*

A sensitive recasting of the ancient tale shows we have the power to deal with anger in positive ways. Provides questions for kids and adults to explore together. "Editor's Choice"—American Library Association's *Booklist* 9 x 12, 32 pp, HC, Full-color illus., ISBN 1-58023-123-3 **$16.95**

In Our Image: *God's First Creatures*

For ages 4 & up

by *Nancy Sohn Swartz;* Full-color illus. by *Melanie Hall*

A playful new twist on the Creation story—from the perspective of the animals. Celebrates the interconnectedness of nature and the harmony of all living things. "The vibrantly colored illustrations nearly leap off the page in this delightful interpretation." —*School Library Journal*

"A message all children should hear, presented in words and pictures that children will find irresistible." —Rabbi Harold Kushner, author of *When Bad Things Happen to Good People*

9 x 12, 32 pp, HC, Full-color illus., ISBN 1-879045-99-0 **$16.95**

Children's Spirituality

ENDORSED BY CATHOLIC, PROTESTANT, JEWISH, AND BUDDHIST RELIGIOUS LEADERS

Because Nothing Looks Like God

by *Lawrence and Karen Kushner*
Full-color illus. by *Dawn W. Majewski*

For ages 4 & up

MULTICULTURAL, NONDENOMINATIONAL, NONSECTARIAN

Real-life examples of happiness and sadness—from goodnight stories, to the hope and fear felt the first time at bat, to the closing moments of life—introduce children to the possibilities of spiritual life. A vibrant way for children—and their adults—to explore what, where, and how God is in our lives.

11 x 8½, 32 pp, HC, Full-color illus., ISBN 1-58023-092-X **$16.95**

Also available: ***Teacher's Guide,*** 8½ x 11, 22 pp, PB, ISBN 1-58023-140-3 **$6.95** **For ages 5–8**

Where Is God? (A Board Book)

by *Lawrence and Karen Kushner;* Full-color illus. by *Dawn W. Majewski*

For ages 0–4

A gentle way for young children to explore how God is with us every day, in every way. Abridged from *Because Nothing Looks Like God* by Lawrence and Karen Kushner and specially adapted to board book format to delight and inspire young readers.

5 x 5, 24 pp, Board, Full-color illus., ISBN 1-893361-17-9 **$7.95**

What Does God Look Like? (A Board Book)

by *Lawrence and Karen Kushner;* Full-color illus. by *Dawn W. Majewski*

For ages 0–4

A simple way for young children to explore the ways that we "see" God. Abridged from *Because Nothing Looks Like God* by Lawrence and Karen Kushner and specially adapted to board book format to delight and inspire young readers.

5 x 5, 24 pp, Board, Full-color illus., ISBN 1-893361-23-3 **$7.95**

How Does God Make Things Happen? (A Board Book)

by *Lawrence and Karen Kushner;* Full-color illus. by *Dawn W. Majewski*

For ages 0–4

A charming invitation for young children to explore how God makes things happen in our world. Abridged from *Because Nothing Looks Like God* by Lawrence and Karen Kushner and specially adapted to board book format to delight and inspire young readers.

5 x 5, 24 pp, Board, Full-color illus., ISBN 1-893361-24-1 **$7.95**

What Is God's Name? (A Board Book)

by *Sandy Eisenberg Sasso;* Full-color illus. by *Phoebe Stone*

For ages 0–4

Everyone and everything in the world has a name. What is God's name? Abridged from the award-winning *In God's Name* by Sandy Eisenberg Sasso and specially adapted to board book format to delight and inspire young readers.

5 x 5, 24 pp, Board, Full-color illus., ISBN 1-893361-10-1 **$7.95**

Children's Spiritual Biography

MULTICULTURAL, NONDENOMINATIONAL, NONSECTARIAN

Ten Amazing People
And How They Changed the World

For ages 7 & up

by *Maura D. Shaw;* Foreword by *Dr. Robert Coles*
Full-color illus. by *Stephen Marchesi*

Black Elk • Dorothy Day • Malcolm X • Mahatma Gandhi • Martin Luther King, Jr. • Mother Teresa • Janusz Korczak • Desmond Tutu • Thich Nhat Hanh • Albert Schweitzer

This vivid, inspirational, and authoritative book will open new possibilities for children by telling the stories of how ten of the past century's greatest leaders changed the world in important ways.

8½, x 11, 48 pp, HC, Full-color illus., ISBN 1-893361-47-0 **$17.95**

A new series: Spiritual Biographies for Young Readers

Thich Nhat Hanh: *Buddhism in Action*

For ages 7 & up

by *Maura D. Shaw;* Full-color illus. by *Stephen Marchesi*

Warm illustrations, photos, age-appropriate activities, and Thich Nhat Hanh's own poems introduce a great man to children in a way they can understand and enjoy. Includes a list of important Buddhist words to know.

6¾ x 8¾, 32 pp, HC, Full-color illus., ISBN 1-893361-87-X **$12.95**

Gandhi: *India's Great Soul*

For ages 7 & up

by *Maura D. Shaw;* Full-color illus. by *Stephen Marchesi*

There are a number of biographies of Gandhi written for young readers, but this is the only one that balances a simple text with illustrations, photographs, and activities that encourage children and adults to talk about how to make changes happen without violence. Introduces children to important concepts of freedom, equality, and justice among people of all backgrounds and religions.

6¾ x 8¾, 32 pp, HC, Full-color illus., ISBN 1-893361-91-8 **$12.95**

Dorothy Day: *A Catholic Life of Action*

For ages 7 & up

by *Maura D. Shaw;* Full-color illus. by *Stephen Marchesi*

Introduces children to one of the most inspiring women of the twentieth century, a down-to-earth spiritual leader who saw the presence of God in every person she met. Includes practical activities, a timeline, and a list of important words to know.

6¾ x 8¾, 32 pp, HC, Full-color illus., ISBN 1-59473-011-3 **$12.99**

Religious Etiquette/Reference

How to Be a Perfect Stranger, 3rd Edition

The Essential Religious Etiquette Handbook

Edited by *Stuart M. Matlins* and *Arthur J. Magida*

The indispensable guidebook to help the well-meaning guest when visiting other people's religious ceremonies.

A straightforward guide to the rituals and celebrations of the major religions and denominations in the United States and Canada from the perspective of an interested guest of any other faith, based on information obtained from authorities of each religion. Belongs in every living room, library, and office.

COVERS:

African American Methodist Churches • Assemblies of God • Baha'i • Baptist • Buddhist • Christian Church (Disciples of Christ) • Christian Science (Church of Christ, Scientist) • Churches of Christ • Episcopalian and Anglican • Hindu • Islam • Jehovah's Witnesses • Jewish • Lutheran • Mennonite/Amish • Methodist • Mormon (Church of Jesus Christ of Latter-day Saints) • Native American/First Nations • Orthodox Churches • Pentecostal Church of God • Presbyterian • Quaker (Religious Society of Friends) • Reformed Church in America/Canada • Roman Catholic • Seventh-day Adventist • Sikh • Unitarian Universalist • United Church of Canada • United Church of Christ

6 x 9, 432 pp, Quality PB, ISBN 1-893361-67-5 **$19.95**

What You Will See Inside A Mosque

by *Aisha Karen Kahn;* Photographs by *Aaron Pepis*

A colorful, fun-to-read introduction that explains the ways and whys of Muslim faith and worship.

Visual and informative, featuring full-page pictures and concise descriptions of what is happening, the objects used, the spiritual leaders and laypeople who have specific roles, and the spiritual intent of the believers.

Ideal for children as well as teachers, partents, librarians, clergy, and lay leaders who want to demystify the celebrations and ceremonies of Islam throughout the year, as well as encourage understanding and tolerance among different faith traditions.

8½ x 10½, 32 pp, Full-color photographs, HC, ISBN 1-893361-60-8 **$16.95**